IF YOU WANT
TO LEAD,
NOT JUST
MANAGE

A PRIMER FOR PRINCIPALS

DENNIS R. DUNKLEE
FOREWORD BY GERALD W. BRACEY

CORWIN PRESS, INC.
A Sage Publications Company
Thousand Oaks, California

For information:

Corwin Press, Inc.
A Sage Publications Company
2455 Teller Road
Thousand Oaks, California 91320
E-mail: order@corwinpress.com

Sage Publications Ltd.
6 Bonhill Street
London EC2A 4PU
United Kingdom

Sage Publications India Pvt. Ltd.
M-32 Market
Greater Kailash I
New Delhi 110 048 India

Printed in the United States of America

Library of Congress Cataloging-in-Publication Data
Dunklee, Dennis R.
    If you want to lead, not just manage : A primer for principals /
by Dennis R. Dunklee.
        p.   cm.
    Includes bibliographical references and index.
    ISBN 0-7619-7646-9 (cloth : alk. paper)
    ISBN 0-7619-7647-7 (pbk. : alk. paper)
    1. School principals—United States—Handbooks, manuals, etc.
    2. Educational leadership—United States—Handbooks, manuals,
    etc.   3. School management and organization—United States—
    Handbooks, manuals, etc.   I. Title.
    LB2831.92 .D85   2000
    371.2'012'0973—dc21   00-008180

00   01   02   03   04   05   06   7   6   5   4   3   2   1

Corwin Editorial Assistant: Kylee Liegl
Production Editor: Denise Santoyo
Editorial Assistant: Victoria Cheng
Typesetter/Designer: Lynn Miyata/Danielle Dillahunt
Cover Designer: Oscar Desierto

Contents

Foreword

People often congratulate me on my "courage" in presenting data that show American public schools to be performing at higher levels than critics claim; indeed, for some variables performing at the highest levels in history. I am aware that going against the grain, standing up for schools, saying the emperor has no clothes, is not a good way to win popularity contests (or grants). But, even so, we researchers mostly get to stand off to one side and watch. We catalogue what *is*—practitioners have to figure out what to do with it. Thus, when people applaud me for my stands, I think of Hemingway's comment, in reference to bullfighting, that the proper place to send our praise is to "the man in the ring."

Principals are the men and women in the ring. The big difference is that they face more than one bull simultaneously. In *If You Want to Lead, Not Just Manage*, Dennis Dunklee provides an excellent guide to make you a skilled educational toreador. Dunklee asks readers to first ask themselves, "Do I really want to be a principal?" There are reasons that will give you pause, for sure. But there are more reasons to move ahead to what Dunklee perceives is a profession that, when performed skillfully, provides a great deal of gratification and satisfaction (if no rest).

Dunklee describes the *corrida* in which the principal must perform. He makes it clear that even though teachers and principals occupy the same buildings, a teacher who becomes a principal invites culture shock because everything that previously seemed so familiar now looks so different. He adeptly describes the conflicts between leadership and allegiance, the difficulty—but ultimately the possibility—of simultaneously being a leader and a manager. He leads the reader through the niceties of wielding influence without it being seen as manipulation, of gaining autonomy in a culture that demands accountability—and doing it within the multiple, often competing cultures that a principal must cope with: students, teachers, secretaries, counselors, librarians, and assistant principals, not to mention the central office, the board of education, and the community.

Your job, Dunklee points out, is merely to "meld these disparate interests into a working unit, attending simultaneously to both individual and institutional needs." And that's not all. As Dunklee views it, principals are "CEO's of small corporations, social workers, cheerleaders, cops, defendants in lawsuits, and, more and more often, fall guys." But, in the end, they are leaders. Happily, this book provides a lively, highly readable, and practical guide to it all.

Dunklee can act as a guide because he's been there: teacher, principal, and central office administrator. The book is written in the voice of "you" and could have been titled "So you want to be a principal." One wonders how Dunklee spent so many years in education and maintained such a vibrant, vivid style. The book is actually a joy to read.

—Gerald W. Bracey,
Author of *The Bracey Report on the Condition of Education,*
and *Bail Me Out! An Educator's Guide to Handling
Tough Questions About Public Schools*

Preface

The privilege—and penalty—of your education is that over the coming decades you will be the pace setters for political and social thought in your communities. You may not accept this responsibility, but that makes no difference. It is inescapable. For if you decide to set no pace, to forward no new ideas, to dream no new dreams, you will still be pace setters. You have already decided that there is to be no pace.

—Adlai E. Stevenson

School principals are no longer just educators. They are the CEOs of small corporations; social workers; cheerleaders; cops; defendants in lawsuits; and, more and more often, fall guys. As a result, fewer people are willing to take the job. "People are looking at these jobs and saying it's not worth it."[1] Today's schools face all the issues of a small city, and principals, like mayors, must answer daily to an anxious community. If you want to become a school principal—a school leader—if you're in the process of struggling through your early years as a school administrator, or even if you're a veteran principal seeking a tool for reflecting on and validating your professional practice, then this book is about you and the things you need to know about the culture of schools and school districts. This book is about you and the things you need to know if you

- Have an impelling urge to make a difference and to make yourself a positive vehicle to effect outcomes in the culture of schools, school districts, and the communities that support them

- Believe that passivity can seldom, if ever, be your watchword. Your password is action and is multidimensional and straightforward

- Have confidence in yourself that will show others that you can be an *effective* leader

This book is about you, the aggregate impression you want others to have of you, and how you can align yourself to fit the administrative culture of schools and school districts if you want to become an effective principal and leader. The essence of effective leadership is the *acceptance of responsibility,* but effective principals interpret this statement as more. They see their role as being prepared to lead by exposure to risk, and they understand that to be effective they must know how much risk they can afford. They also know that inherent in this acceptance is an inclusive *understanding of the culture in which they lead.* They know that without some grasp of their relationship to the whole—the culture in which they want to succeed—it will be impossible for them to retain a clear sense of their own capacities to act as individuals. Effective principals strive to be individuals who demonstrate full awareness of their true role and inherent responsibilities. If they fail at this, they recognize that they will be forced to accept a spectator role or sink into passivity.

So, this book is about you if you

- Believe that some of your ideas, and even some of your fantasies, can make a difference in the course of events. You believe that change can never be a sideline for you in the role of leader—that it's one of the basic activities in which you must engage. You understand that to describe a person who strives to maintain the status quo as a leader is a contradiction in terms.

- Understand that real power doesn't lie in documents and memos, rules and regulations, policies and procedures that delineate your terms of reference and area of jurisdiction: *It lies in what you can achieve in practice—it lies with the people for whom you serve.*

In the textbook world, schools and school districts are often described as a culture that places high value on, and supports and enhances, openness, high trust, caring, and sharing; that always strives for consensus but supports and values those who think differently; and that advocates human growth and development. But that's in the textbook world. In the real world of schools and school districts, there's a significant difference, at least in the domain of the principalship. As a principal, you can achieve the textbook definition, but you'll have to earn and maintain that right. This book will help you find the *starting line* for your quest. If you're serious about becoming an effective principal, however, be advised that you are about to enter a race without a *finish line*.

To get a broader picture of how a typical principal blends the disparate roles described in this book, I respectfully direct the reader to another book, a case study, that dovetails the real-world concepts presented in this book with real-world, day-to-day practice. The recommended case study follows a principal's professional life from initial assignment through retirement. The book (case study), published by Corwin Press in 1999, is *You Sound Taller on the Telephone: A Practitioner's View of the Principalship* (Dunklee, 1999).

And the pilot—that is to say, the true pilot—is he a captain of sailors or a mere sailor?

A captain of sailors.

The circumstance that he sails in the ship is not to be taken into account; neither is he to be called a sailor; the name pilot by which he is distinguished has nothing to do with sailing, but is significant of his skill and of his authority over the sailors.

—Plato, *The Republic*

NOTE

1. L. Waples, principal of Glassmore Elementary School, Oxon Hill, Maryland, cited in Perlstein (1991, p. B1).

REFERENCES

Dunklee, D. R. (1999). *You sound taller on the telephone: A practitioner's view of the principalship.* Thousand Oaks, CA: Corwin.
Perlstein, L. (1991, January 5). Wanted: A few good principals. *Washington Post*, p. B1.

About the Author

Dennis R. Dunklee received his PhD in school administration and foundations from Kansas State University. His major area of research was in the field of education law, and his dissertation was on tort liability for negligence. He holds a bachelor's degree in elementary and secondary vocal and instrumental music education from Wichita State University and a master's degree in elementary and secondary school administration from Washburn University. During his 25 years in public schools, he served as a teacher, elementary school principal, junior high/middle school principal, high school principal, and central office administrator. He has been at George Mason University since 1986 and is an Associate Professor in the Education Leadership Department in the Graduate School of Education. He teaches courses in education law, school administration, and school business management, and serves as an advisor/chair for master's and doctoral candidates in school leadership as well as in community college leadership. Because of his expertise and practical experience, he is frequently called on as a consultant in the areas of effective schools, school law, administrator evaluation, instructional supervision, school-community relations, problem solving, and conflict resolution. In addition, he has been involved as a consultant and expert witness in numerous school-related lawsuits nationwide. As a university scholar and researcher, he has published 4 textbooks,

2 monographs, and more than 75 articles on issues in the fields of school law, business management, administrative practice, and leadership theory. He is active in a number of professional organizations; has presented papers at national, regional, state, and local conferences; and is a widely sought-after clinician for in-service workshops.

This is Dr. Dunklee's second book for Corwin Press. His first Corwin book, *You Sound Taller on the Telephone: A Practitioner's View of the Principalship* was published in 1999.

**CORWIN
PRESS**

The Corwin Press logo—a raven striding across an open book—represents the happy union of courage and learning. We are a professional-level publisher of books and journals for K–12 educators, and we are committed to creating and providing resources that embody these qualities. Corwin's motto is "Success for All Learners."

Introduction

And there were three men
Went down the road as down the road went he:
The man they saw,
The man he was,
The man he wanted to be.

—John Masefield

Assuming that you're a prospective or newly established school principal, or even a veteran principal reflecting on your own professional practice, then this book is all about you and the unique behaviors you will need to understand, adopt, and constantly renew to become an effective principal. This book is unusual in that it deals specifically with the things you need to know and understand about yourself and others and about the sociological nature of the principalship. It is a significant departure from traditional books about the principalship in a number of ways.

Pre- and in-service principal programs are commonly built on a foundation of learning about the principalship primarily in terms of manager/technician (What do I do? How do I do it?). As a result, typical pre- and in-service programs focus on budgeting skills, personnel procedures and supervision, a capacity to diagnose problems in organizational communications, litigation avoidance, risk management, and competence in research and evaluation techniques. Mastering such skills is important and clearly necessary, as the technical skills needed to function successfully in today's schools are extensive. But such training often lacks a serious attempt to teach about the principalship as an art (How am I supposed to act? How do I look?). The three main categories of skills (minimum competencies) that new or prospective administrators/principals need to master to be successful are (a) technical skills related to new roles (What do I do?), (b) socialization skills (How am I supposed to look and act?), and (c) self-awareness skills (How do I look? How do I appear to others?) (Daresh & Playko, 1995).

An education that provides a prospective principal with technical/managerial skills but fails to teach anything substantial about the social survival skills applicable to administering schools is seriously incomplete and leads to—well, see for yourself. Here's a list, compiled from a number of different reports, of the most common reasons why school administrators fail:

- Lack of integrity
- Lack of respect for other administrators
- Failure to maintain confidentiality
- Lack of cooperation (subordination rather than cooperation)
- Failure to lead
- Failure to manage
- Failure to be accessible
- Failure to communicate
- Failure to comply with ethical and moral standards
- Failure to adapt to political changes
- Failure to manage funds (mismanagement)

Note that only 1 of the 11 items listed calls for specific technical/managerial expertise—the management of funds. The remaining 10 illustrate a variety of social/behavioral skills—the *art* of school administration and the primary focus of this book.

Along with the examination of the *socialization and self-awareness* skills you need to be effective in the principalship, this book examines *technical* skills from a different angle. Not what do I do to solve this particular problem, but rather, what do I do to fit into the organization in such a way that I have the freedom to solve problems, period—and succeed? How can I become a leader, as opposed to a technician, in the education enterprise? What do I need to do or understand to acquire a panoramic view of the forest (the culture) rather than maintain a simplistic and telescopic focus on a single tree? John Gardner, who later became Secretary of Health, Education, and Welfare and the founder of Common Cause, noted in his final report as president of the Carnegie Corporation, "The academic world appears to be approaching a point at which everyone will want to educate the technical expert who advises the leader, but no one will want to educate the leader himself" (1965, p. 12). This book emphasizes leadership competence rather than technical skill.

We know that the principalship is, by all accounts, a critical position in creating an effective school. Among researchers and practitioners in school administration, however, the principalship has remained an enigma. No matter what type of scrutiny the job is exposed to, no matter what kinds of how-to books are written about the position, the lack of symmetry between theory and practice and the lack of clearly defined differences between real and perceived expectations continue to evade conclusive direction, much less definition. During the past decade or so, a number of studies have confirmed the conventional wisdom, which holds that the climate and effectiveness of a particular school are influenced by the leadership and management that a principal provides. But as any effective principal knows, students, parents, teachers, central office administrators, and others consistently differ in their perceptions of, and expectations for, principals, and these differences make the principalship an extremely complex position. The nature and implications of these differences have been the subject of much conjecture, as have the ways that principals can and should deal with them. Before you can deal with them, however, you must understand your position in the social/political/business hierarchy. It's not the position that determines whether someone is a leader, it is the nature of that individual's behavior while occupying that position (Lipman, 1964). This book provides some thought-provoking answers, along sociological/behavioral lines, to help close the gap between theory and practice and between real and perceived expectations.

Because a lot of what we learn about the principalship comes from those who have been practitioners (myself included), there is a tendency to pass along folklore and tradition. Perhaps this book will

provide you with some of the know-how it takes to create and implement change and to take calculated risks. Consider "folklore" versus
"risk" as you read the following:

> Some behavioral scientists put five monkeys in a room with
> a pole, atop which rests some bananas. There are shower
> heads in the ceiling. Every time a monkey climbs the pole for
> bananas, scientists douse the room with cold water. Those
> monkeys learn not to climb the pole. Then scientists send in
> new monkeys that don't know any better.
>
> This time, the scientists don't have to use water to stop
> the monkeys from going for the bananas because whenever
> they try, the first group beats the daylights out of them to
> avoid getting drenched themselves. Eventually the room
> has a whole new group of monkeys that won't dare touch
> the pole, even though the original deterrent is a mystery to
> them. . . .
>
> We will not graduate monkeys here . . .you must come
> out thinking critically about decisions and being able to
> question the way things are done, because you may see
> something that's stupid and worth changing.[1]

Leadership is a process rather than a personal attribute, and the
leadership process begins with an understanding of the social order
and the nature of human behavior in the overall education hierarchy.
"True education emerges from an understanding of the social order
and the nature of man, and from no other source" (Sizer, 1996, p. 8).
To be an effective leader, you must be able to see the social environment in which you will attempt to lead. In addition, you must be able
to understand your own behavior and that of multiple constituents.
Leadership in education organizations is a situational phenomenon.
It's determined by the collective perceptions of individuals, related
to group norms, and influenced by the frequency of interaction
among members of the organization. Before leadership can be effective in open organizations such as schools, it must be acknowledged
as a group activity.

As an effective education leader, you must understand how
education organizations allocate responsibilities among positions,

how each position eventuates in a role, how roles are delimited by expectations, and how expectations affect behavior. To meet these ends, this book is divided into nine interlocking chapters. Each chapter focuses on the building blocks of the environment and culture that a principal needs to understand to establish a leadership base and to be effective.

Two important notes are presented here so that a friendly understanding (not necessarily an agreement) between me and the reader exists when I use the phrase *effective principal*. I have specific definitions in mind when the words *principal* and *effective* appear in this book. First the easy one: The word principal, wherever used, denotes *all* of the multiple roles expected of the position, for example, leader, manager, counselor, cheerleader, administrator, keeper of the keys. The word effective, when placed before the title principal, is not so easy to define and provokes continuing scholarly discussion between practitioners and theorists and between theorists and theorists. For the purpose of this book, I borrow from the law and its definition of a *reasonable and prudent person*. Courts have long defined this person, under legal tenets, as a person who is unlike even any jury member who would be called on to serve in judgment of another. This reasonable and prudent person, under the law, is a figment of one's imagination, an ideal picture that one would, or could, conjure up to represent a "perfect" person in a particular role. So, (a) an effective principal is, at least, a reasonable and prudent person to this observer—there is no "perfect"—and (b) an effective principal leads a school and the profession forward—always keeping a primary focus on mission, improvement, and distinction. A satisfactory principal is only effective in managing the status quo; an unsatisfactory principal isn't considered in this book.

NOTE

1. U.S. Marine Corps Col. Robert E. Lee, speaking to a leadership training session for Southwest Airlines Company employees, cited in McKay (1998, pp. G1, G9).

REFERENCES

Daresh, J. C., & Playko, M. A. (1995, March). *Alternative career forma-tion perspectives: Lessons for educational leadership from law, medi-cine, and priesthood.* Paper presented at the annual meeting of the University Council for Educational Administration, Salt Lake City, UT.

Gardner, J. W. (1965). *Final report as president of the Carnegie Corpora-tion.* New York: Carnegie Corporation.

Lipman, R. T. (1964). Leadership and administration. In D. Griffiths (Ed.), *Behavioral science and educational administration* (63rd year-book of the National Society for the Study of Education). Chi-cago: University of Chicago Press.

McKay, P. A. (1998, December 5). Leadership, in war or at the air-port. *Washington Post*, pp. G1, G9.

Sizer, T. (1996). *Horace's hope: What works for the American high school.* Boston: Houghton Mifflin.

1

Culture Shock

When Teachers Become Principals

ABOUT THIS CHAPTER

As a school principal, you must understand typical school districts' internal cultures and how superiors, employees, patrons, and students define the distinct culture of the principalship. This chapter introduces you to the culture surrounding the position of principal—how that culture places a principal in a role, how that role is delineated by clearly defined *objectives,* and how less well-defined *expectations* affect the behavior of a principal.

The chapter also asks you, after an introduction to some often-underemphasized realities of the principalship, how compatible your personal attributes (nature, character, personality, temperament, qualifications, etc.) may be with the role of an *effective* principal.

REFLECTIVE POINT

Starting to build a general impression—leading to the
aggregate impression others have of you

The way that other people perceive you is likely to influence their interpretation of your behavior and the course of their future interactions with you. Understanding the person perception process takes on considerable significance in the development of a school principal.

When we meet a person for the first time, we begin to form a general impression almost immediately. Although such a general impression may be inaccurate, we still develop a sense of (a) whether we like or dislike the person, and (b) what the person's personality and traits are. This first encounter is the starting point of forming our aggregate impression of the other person.

The cognitive process involved in the acquisition of information about others and in making judgments about them is identified by social psychologists as a person's information-processing approach. The question is, at this point, what do others think of you? What is their aggregate impression of you?

ROLE PREPARATION

Setting the Stage

Very few children, when asked the question, "So, what do you want to be when you grow up?", declare that they want to be a school principal. "A teacher, maybe," is a fairly common response, along with "firefighter," "nurse," or "astronaut," but seldom would you expect them to aspire to be "the principal." Likewise, very few teachers, on entering the profession, think about the principalship as a career goal. Yet most—actually, almost all—of our nation's middle- and upper-level administrators are recruited from the ranks of teachers. Somewhere in their teaching careers they decide, for diverse reasons, to take coursework in school administration to qualify for informal leadership or managerial roles that develop in the school setting. As a result of exposure in these roles, they may be identified by their superiors as potential administrators.

School principals chosen from the teaching ranks bring with them the knowledge of the classroom environment, the scuttlebutt of the teacher's lounge, the barking of the teachers' union's continuing demands and the equally strident response from the board of education, and the book learning from their university coursework. During their years as classroom teachers, they have generally been confined to a single room with 30 desks; appropriate blackboard and bulletin board space; audiovisual supplies and materials; a teacher's desk and chair; and, most important, a four-drawer file cabinet (add stopwatches for coaches, metronomes for music teachers, blank tape cassettes for foreign language specialists, etc.). Regardless of their teaching specialty, their austere budget has probably been controlled by a vigilant main office secretary who limits the number of pencils, paper clips, and sheets of paper they can have; their professional life has been directed and controlled by principals; and their private life has been continuously measured against the mores of the community.

Now, with this limited professional and personal background, do teachers have the prerequisites for an administrative appointment? Interestingly, many do—if they have

- Astutely observed the way the school functions beyond the confines of their particular classroom
- Studied their principals and observed how their fellow teachers react to the multitude of events that take place during a typical school day
- Tried to understand the rationale behind administrative decisions and examined the effects of politics on their school and school district
- Attempted to move their sphere of practical knowledge from the classroom to the principal's office and beyond
- Developed a strong résumé (think *marketing*) that gives any reader a picture of them as potential professional manager/ leaders who demonstrate, on paper, the kinds of experiences that merit consideration for the principalship

And of course, if they've

- Taken themselves beyond the job description—come in a little earlier, left a little later. And they've understood that even though they've earned the proper degrees and certification, and even landed a job in that really great school district they've dreamed about, before they can save the world, they have to learn what tools to use. Let's use an analogy from another profession for a moment. You may have envisioned yourself wearing the crisp white chef's hat as you head off to work at the city's swankiest restaurant. But when you've heard a call for a batch of cheeseburgers and a few orders of fries, you've taken a deep breath and flipped the burgers. You've understood that you had to be a line cook before you could become a master chef. And you've used the line cook job as a fabulous opportunity to show off in a lot of different ways.

And finally, one sure indicator that teachers may have the right stuff to be effective school principals is whether, while still in the role of teacher, they have consistently been able to get more than one pencil at a time from the secretarial guardian of the supply cabinet.

Now, will potential followers rise up and identify a teacher as a person they would like to work for? It seldom happens. The route to the principalship is so circuitous that we can't prescribe, much less identify, a typical route. If we try to distinguish a particular pattern, myriad factors—including an individual's specific abilities, visibility, timing, willingness, fortuitous circumstance, influential persons, specific situations, or pure luck of the draw—are sure to emerge. The existence of identifiable stepping-stones to the principalship may be more imagined than real. One factor identified above seems to stand out: When a teacher is willing to tackle problems or perform tasks that are clearly outside or beyond the expectations of immediate supervisors, others may consider this a display of leadership potential. The questions to be asked, then, are, is this willingness rooted in the person's desire to be recognized as an ambitious employee? Is it based on an individual's personal competence? Is this a person who is not only willing, but more important, able?

We should note that a common route to the principalship is exposure as an assistant principal or in quasi-administrative jobs such as special program director, a temporary staff assignment at the district office, or some kind of an internship or administrative aide position. In addition, and perhaps most important, is the support of a mentor—someone already in an administrative position in the school district. If you can catch the eye of a highly regarded administrator, already identified by superiors as effective, who will adopt you or take you under his or her wing, such a mentor can provide valuable in-service training and become a key player in supporting your advancement.

Visibility

Visibility is a critical step in gaining the support of a mentor. Visibility is defined in terms of what you do, who knows you, who you know, and how alert you have been to organizational needs. How well you do your job is certainly the starting point for personal visibility and leads directly to who knows you, either by direct contact or by reputation. And of course, many a career has been founded on getting to know the right people. Your visibility is really heightened if you can place yourself in the limelight because you sensed, expressed, and addressed needs when other organizational members were conscious of the issues but little or nothing was being done. Identifying such needs, being able to describe them, and articulating reasonable courses of action to resolve them is an excellent way to attract visibility. To gain a mentor's eye is only a first step, however. Ensuring a mentor's support for promotion to an administrative position will involve a close match between your *readiness* (promotability), your *reputation* (visibility), and the *political strength* (network status) of your mentor. If this triangular match occurs, you'll probably get your promotion.

Unfortunately, principals are rarely chosen by the group they will lead. Instead, a principal is identified, appointed, and given control by a board of education or trustees—people who are not subject to the appointed administrator's control; have seldom, if ever, worked with the appointee; and, more often than not, make appointments based on some combination of the circumstances listed above. Regardless of how you may be selected, as a principal you are immediately expected to fill the role of manager and leader. And although you may have read about the role, taken appropriate coursework, and played at the game of boss, your potential success is nearly always a gamble. Responsibility for the management and leadership process resides solely with you. It is not something that a board can decree. The traits of an effective principal, including the abilities to manage and lead, are difficult to teach and impossible to mandate. Such abilities or traits must be acquired.

So, after all this, when the superintendent recommends someone for a principalship and the board of education appoints a principal, they believe they have selected a person who is willing to accept the position and apparently has the ability to assume the responsibility. They believe they have appointed a person who is willing to be highly visible, to chance the career risk that might be involved, and to bear the consequences if that individual's qualifications should prove insufficient or abilities to solve problems inadequate. The board has concluded that the chosen candidate has the conceptual, anthropological, and technical skills necessary to be successful as a school principal.[1] The board also assumes that the objectives of the job have been clearly defined. But have they? Or are there "expectations" that have not been so clearly defined—or not defined at all?

Understanding a New Role With Clearly Defined Objectives as Well as Less Well-Defined Expectations

Once you are offered and accept the position of principal, your behavior is prescribed to a great extent. Because the principal has observable public responsibility and authority, because of the tenuous nature of the position, because of the certain status and the rewards that it brings, vested observers both inside and outside the school expect the accomplishment of specific objectives and hold certain expectations of you, regardless of who you are. A principal's behavior is largely prescribed and socially restricted by other individuals' and groups' clearly defined *objectives*. But these clearly defined objectives may, in fact, contradict the less well-defined *expectations* of the same individuals and groups. Effective principals quickly learn how to balance the demand for the achievement of objectives and the meeting of expectations. For example, the superintendent and the board expect you to require your faculty and staff to strictly adhere to the district's rules, regulations, policies, and procedures. And although you understand that such adherence is absolutely necessary, you are deeply concerned about keeping faculty and staff morale at the highest peak possible. "I'm sorry, Mr. Smith . . . I can't allow . . . I can't have your classes covered for you, or get a substitute, for your (Pick one: doctor's appointment, the closing on your new house, best friend's out-of-town wedding, etc.). District policy clearly states . . . therefore, you'll have to . . . ." The objectives of the school district are clear-cut: "Thou shalt not . . . ." Your faculty and staff's expectations of you are never clear-cut, and these people look to you for leniency. After all, they assume, policies should be tempered with human sensitivity.

Table 1.1

Clearly Defined Objectives		*Less Well-Defined Expectations*
High student achievement	*however*	High student morale No vandalism Winning athletic teams
Strong community support	*however*	No late-night phone calls to the superintendent or board members Winning athletic teams No negative publicity
Clean, safe facilities and grounds	*however*	Within prescribed budget and with existing custodial staff
Effective student discipline	*however*	Not too many suspensions or expulsions No late-night phone calls to the superintendent or board members Winning athletic teams
Exemplar status as principal	*however*	Keep your private life private
Keep the lid on the place; follow rules, regulations, policies, and procedures	*however*	Leaders take risks No surprises Vertical allegiance No late-night phone calls to the superintendent or board members

So, you will be held responsible for any and all clearly defined objectives. You will, however—and "however" is the operative word here—be held equally accountable for those often unspoken, less well-defined expectations. Table 1.1 shows some examples of objectives and expectations—linked by the caveat "however."

In addition to maintaining a balance between clearly defined objectives and the less well-defined expectations, to be an effective principal you'll also have to balance an additional set of forces. Principals, just like any other effective leaders, need to express their indi-

Table 1.2

Sanctions/Expectations	Individuality/Personalization
Formal organization	Informal relationships
By the book	Flexible/situational decision making
Required	Optional
The district view	The school/community view
Winning	Encouraging participation
Positive test scores	Fostering student growth
Perceived role	Real role
Linear behavior	Nonlinear behavior

viduality by personalizing their schools. Some might compare this phenomenon to a cat marking its territory. Principals are expected, however, to exhibit the behavior that others anticipate—in other words, to play a role. Effective principals engage in a continual tug-of-war between school district sanctions and expectations on one hand and their own individuality and desire for personalization on the other. See the examples in Table 1.2.

And finally, principals share the challenge we all face of simple communication. The source of the challenge lies in the fact that each of us, as sender as well as receiver, has a reference point for any type of communication and unconsciously assumes that others have the same reference point. In addition, each of us has a set of inherent values that we believe are right. In other words, communication, simply defined, is a process through which an individual or group receives a sense impression of the message of another. The operative words here are *receive, sense,* and *impression.* An effective principal's referent is tempered by the ability to foresee how a particular message might be received after the recipient has filtered the message through a set of personal or perceptual screens.[2]

Stephen Covey (1989) suggests that senders should "seek first to understand and then to be understood." Concerning recipients, he observes, "Most people do not listen with the intent to understand: They listen with the intent to reply. They're filtering everything through their own paradigms, reading their autobiography into other people's lives" (p. 239).

Effective communicators ensure that any message they send is as close as possible to what they believe is the mind-set of the receiver. For example, as receivers we generally favor a message we perceive to be similar to what we already believe. The greater the differences, cultural mores, environmental situation, religious beliefs, and so on between sender and receiver, the greater the barrier to effective communication. What does this mean? Empathy, authenticity, credibility, foreseeability, and role adaptation are all key to an effective principal's ability to deal with the highly diverse student, parent, faculty, and staff population evident in any school. In Chapter 5, we'll take a closer look at the *art* of effective listening.

So, Now—Welcome to the Fishbowl

To this point, you've been introduced to some of the often-underemphasized realities of administrative life in the school setting—more are coming. But now you should think about what you want from the position. The odds of long-term success seem to be better if you seek satisfaction of *motivation* needs, that is, "I want to do this," or a combination of motivation and *perceptual* needs, that is, "I can do this," than when you are driven by *maintenance* needs alone, that is, "I want the money, power, and so on." In other words, if you seek or are in the principalship for maintenance needs alone, then success could be fleeting. Some of the questions you might want to consider now, and revisit once in a while throughout your principalship, are

- Am I willing to work and find satisfaction under the constraints school principals experience?
- Can I deal with the expectations of individuals and groups both inside and outside the education enterprise, fishbowl visibility, and pressures from individuals and groups with vested interests?
- Can I adjust my everyday behavior to fit the role of a school principal?
- Can I effectively deal with the tension between individuality and conformity, value conflicts, or role conflicts?

- Can I relate to the diverse audiences that I will be addressing each day?

And finally,

- Can I find ways to improve the process of education and education administration, take calculated risks, and still fit the role as described so far in this book?

Getzels, Lipham, and Campbell (1968) noted,

> A role has certain normative rights and duties, which we may call role expectations. When the role incumbent puts these rights and duties in effect, he is said to be performing in his role. The expectations define what the actor, whoever he may be, should or should not do under various circumstances while occupying the particular role in the social system. (p. 112)

So, the real question might be, are you ready to assume or continue a major acting role in a very difficult play with a diverse and demanding audience? If your answer is yes—even if it's hesitant as opposed to emphatic—then read on. If your answer is no—that's still a positive response and you're urged to continue. Here's why. A university professor, when anonymously reviewing an early draft of this book, stated,

> When I first started teaching the principalship, if a student expressed doubts about becoming a principal, I could feel myself almost pushing that student away—not giving that student my full attention. Over the years, I've had a change of mind. Now when I hear doubts, I gravitate to those students hoping that they might represent individuals with a "new" vision of principaling: individuals not consumed by ambition and self-promotion and school system socialization.

So, regardless of your answer, please read on.

Table 1.3

Acquires	Designs	Keeps	Provides
Appraises	Encourages	Knows	Recognizes
Assists	Establishes	Maintains	Requires
Avoids	Fosters	Models	Reviews
Budgets	Furthers	Organizes	Schedules
Communicates	Helps	Participates	Understands
Conducts	Identifies	Plans	Uses
Continues	Implements	Practices	Works with
Delineates	Initiates	Processes	Writes
Demonstrates	Involves	Produces	

When You're in Charge,
Life Becomes an Action Verb

Now that you're in the role, (insert appropriate verb) the job as best you can. Let's (insert appropriate verb) your performance. When we (insert appropriate verb) the performance criteria for principals across the country, one message (insert appropriate verb) clear. Your evaluation (insert appropriate verb) based entirely in the linguistic/grammatical world of verbs, or at least it seems like it is.[3] School districts traditionally judge the work of principals using descriptors like those listed in Table 1.3.

This list is really a principal's job description sans other parts of speech. For example, a typical evaluation statement might read: The principal *provides* an environment of trust that is responsive to the collective needs of students, parents, patrons, faculty, and staff. Here is another example: The principal *initiates* programs to ensure continuous progress toward raising the school's standardized test scores. The question asked by the principal's supervisor/evaluator would be, has the principal *demonstrated* competency in these areas of evaluation? This is the way a typical school district measures/evaluates the clearly defined objectives previously mentioned. It's not too different from a teacher's evaluation. But in the case of principals, we can't forget the importance of the previously mentioned less well-defined expectations.

Ambiguity, anxiety, and uncertainty all describe the feelings of principals who try to figure out what they really need to do to earn a positive evaluation from patrons, peers, and superiors. Effective principals quickly learn that the balancing of their behavior with the less well-defined expectations of patrons, peers, and superiors coupled with continuous progress toward the clearly defined objectives of the same groups will generally result in a positive evaluation. Bottom line: Effective principals watch their p's and q's, and—a whole lot of action verbs. A principal doesn't just exist and fill a role or an office chair. An effective principal *acts.*

Oh, and lest we forget, there's more—a principal's job description usually includes the following final statement: "and any or all other assignments as designated by the Superintendent or Board of Education."

The Real You, the Perceived You— and the Administrative Role

Preschool or primary school-age children commonly proclaim, "When I grow up, I want to be just like . . . !" Intermediate school-age children will tell you, "Sure, I have a role model!" Adolescents ask the mirror, "I wonder how others see me?" and a young adult might state, "I am who I am!" Just like the child and young adult you once were, as a principal you need to learn how compatible the person *you want to be* is with the person *you are,* and the person *others see;* how compatible your personal attributes (nature, character, personality, temperament, qualifications, etc.) are with the role of principal; how compatible your personal expectations and perceptions are with those of others.

In determining whether or not you are suited to the rigor of a principalship and the adversity of leadership and management, you must consider the perceptions of you held by others. Certainly, these perceptions have an influence on whether you'll even be given the opportunity to serve in a role in which the varied functions of principal could be realized—much less, fulfilled. The importance of others' perceptions of you, and how they can positively or adversely affect your ability to perform as an administrator, will be examined later in a discussion of leadership qualities. In the meantime, let's assume that your personal attributes seem to fit the role of an effective principal—you can see yourself functioning successfully in the role, and you believe that others see you in the same way.

The Cultures of the Elementary, Middle, and High School Principalship Compared

At this point, let's take a brief look at the distinct roles of elementary, middle school, and high school principals—are they really as distinct as we tend to think? For starters, let's agree (Assumption 1) that in most school districts, high schools usually have a larger enrollment, have larger buildings and grounds, and programmatically in both curricular and extracurricular respects are more complex than elementary schools. Middle schools are usually just that, *in the middle* between high school and elementary school demographics.

Let's also agree (Assumption 2) that extracurricular activities increase exponentially from level to level starting at the elementary school. The high school principal's professional life is crowded with night and weekend activities and accompanying responsibilities. Although the elementary school principal has some night and weekend activities, the numbers are far less. Again, the middle school principal is in the middle, with more activities than an elementary school, fewer than a high school.

Now, it's clearly difficult to disagree with the two assumptions mentioned above. These same assumptions are often used as the premise for a third assumption, however, namely, that each level, starting with the elementary school, is exponentially more difficult to manage. This assumption is erroneous unless difficulty is measured strictly against demographics, student maturity, and activities. Here's a sound-bite for your consideration:

> *High School Principal:* "My students are older, more savvy about adult ways, and as a result often question their teachers' knowledge and authority. They're constantly testing the system and pushing to be seen as adults even though they still act like adolescents."

> *Middle School Principal:* "Well, I could say the same thing about my students. Plus, at this age, they're also rebelling against all sorts of authority, especially their parents."

High School Principal: "Yeah, but mine are physically larger, and clearly more clever and devious. My students threaten my school's stability more than either of yours do."

Middle School Principal: "At least, yours are predictable. Mine are actively going through puberty, which means that each day is totally unpredictable, at least in terms of discipline and maintaining any kind of routine in my office."

High School Principal: "Well, at least you two have the time to serve as an education leader in your schools. I'm required to do that while also directing a kind of police force, whose task it is to keep students in line, maintain surveillance over their behavior, and take corrective action when necessary."

Middle School Principal: "And you don't think I have to play the same role?"

High School Principal: "Many of my parents look to my school to govern their child's conduct, recognizing that they have lost control of them at home."

Middle School Principal: "Same situation here!"

High School Principal: "Okay, here's the bottom line. I'm responsible for keeping these kids off the streets and out of the labor market. I'm responsible for the constant policing of their conduct. I'm responsible for helping my students map out their futures, their careers. My people spend a lot of time hand-holding with students who fret about their futures, their grades, their boyfriends and girlfriends, teachers who don't like them, and parents who don't understand. I'm the entertainment center for the community with sports activities, concerts, plays, pageants, bazaars, homecomings, proms, you name it!"

Middle School Principal: "I do the same thing! I don't see a whole lot of difference between your responsibilities and mine."

Elementary School Principal: "Just out of curiosity, because I don't really want to be involved in this rather frivolous debate— do either of you spend a lot of time consoling parents when they drop their kids off for their first day in kindergarten? Do you worry about such trivial things as an infestation of head lice? Do you have to personally deal with most day-to-day problems from start to finish, or do you delegate many of your tasks to other administrators, counselors, or aides in your respective buildings? Do you receive daily phone calls from parents who are just plain worried about their kids not sleeping well or having nightmares, or lying, or being moody, or constantly sick to their tummies? Are you on call to report to a classroom with very little notice to observe a group of students' 'proud products' or to squeeze yourself into a pint-size chair and read *The Little Engine That Could* or *If You Give a Moose a Muffin* or something like that to a group of kindergarten or primary school kids?"

Okay, end of sound-bite! Now, what did you learn? High school principals have larger egos? Middle school principals have arrested development issues? Elementary school principals are not ergonomically built for their jobs? Note that the three participants in the discussion above concentrated mainly on student maturity issues. This is really the only difference between levels other than the two assumptions already agreed on: size of physical plant and numbers of extracurricular activities. In reality, all three levels share the same leadership and management challenges. The difficulty level is not exponential, it's the same. Kids mature throughout their K-12 experiences and educators at each level—elementary, middle, and high school—have to deal with any and all problems that develop naturally as kids mature. The fundamental leadership/management qualities that define the overall effectiveness of principals are the same.

THE BOTTOM LINE

An inventory of your efforts to prepare for, or continue in, the role of principal demonstrates that you

- Have managed to find the right stepping-stones
- Understand the difference between objectives and expectations

- Are willing to trade some of your individual desires for the sanctions of a difficult role
- Have the required, as well as the acquired, prerequisites, and understand the kinds of communication gaps you will encounter
- Are motivated and willing to take risks while your efforts are measured by verbs
- Are assuming, for now, that your personal attributes seem to fit the role of an effective principal and that you believe that others, through their aggregate impression of you, agree

Now, can you really be effective as the principal of a school? Principals, in search of an answer to this question, first understand that they are part of a middle management team and that their major support mechanism originates at the district level, not at the school level. Effective principals start by looking at the bigger picture and asking, how do I relate to a group of peers at the district level? How does the administrative culture fit within the organization and culture of a typical school district? What is the environment I'm in?

NOTES

1. Conceptual, anthropological, and technical skills will be discussed more fully in Chapter 6.

2. Perceptual screens and "filtering" will be discussed more fully in Chapters 5 and 6.

3. . . . doing. . . . evaluate. . . . examine. . . . is. . . . is.

REFERENCES

Covey, S. R. (1989). *The seven habits of highly effective people.* New York: Simon & Schuster.

Getzels, J. W., Lipham, J. M., & Campbell, R. F. (1968). Institutional expectations. In *Educational administration as a social process* (Chap. 7, pp. 182-217). New York: Harper & Row.

2

Stranger in a Strange Land

The School Environment

ABOUT THIS CHAPTER

School districts, like any other organization or agency, tend to establish an organizational pattern to assure some degree of permanency. ("This is the way we do things here—this is the way we've always done it.") School districts divide labor along hierarchical lines and establish positions that indicate a specific division of labor. They formalize the distinct tasks to be performed in each position, regardless of who the incumbent is, and develop expectations for the behavior of individuals in specific roles. Incumbents are measured/evaluated by their attempts to fulfill assigned tasks and maintain organizational mores and their gains in the achievement of district objectives and goals. Each incumbent plays a role scripted by the expectations of the district.

The principal, as defined in the Introduction to this book, is the administrator, manager, leader of a particular school. But the principal can never be a completely autonomous professional like a doctor or lawyer, but is part of and necessarily responsive to an organizational hierarchy. To faculty and staff at the school site, the principal is the boss. To the board of education, superintendent, and central office staff, the principal is just another employee occupying one of the lower rungs on the managerial ladder. The abbreviated flowchart in Figure 2.1 presents a sample organizational structure for a relatively small to medium-size school district. Larger school districts will have more branches of, and personnel in, the bureaucracy. Smaller school districts might have fewer positions on their organizational chart—but the basic tasks remain the same regardless of the size of a school district. *Note the placement of principals.* This chapter explores the culture of typical school districts and provides some of the insight necessary for you to understand, adapt to, and navigate in this unique culture.

REFLECTIVE POINT

Primary Impression—The first step toward the aggregate impression of you that you want others to have

If we meet or observe a person only once, we may never develop an impression beyond the initial general one. But when we expect to interact with a person over time, we want as much information about the person as possible. We immediately begin to augment our general impression (Chapter 1) by making inferences about what else is likely to be true about that person. This phenomenon occurs regularly in the person perception process. Our inferences are "true" for us and will have an important bearing on our immediate perceptions of the other person.

As we get to know a person better, we acquire more information (e.g., style of interaction, outside interests, aspirations, concerns, as well as perceived strengths and weaknesses or insecurities). With the acquisition of new information about a person, we develop primary impressions that modify and elaborate our general perception of what the person is like that can influence judgments we make about the person. Your understanding of, and your ability to incorporate the information presented in this chapter, will continue to enhance others' aggregate impressions of you.

CHARACTERISTICS OF SCHOOL DISTRICTS

I, (insert full name here), understand that I am expected to, and *pledge* that I will accept the division of labor and responsibility, make myself *subordinate* to the school district and its goals, participate in organizational decision making on a *rational* basis, maintain organizational confidentiality, submit to and legitimize authority, seek personal and professional satisfaction in cooperation with but never at the *expense* of peers, and *accept* centralized control of my actions and initiatives.

Now, with this commitment in mind and dominating all of my future actions, I will go forth as a new principal and become an effective agent of the school district and, most important, an effective principal at my assigned school.

| _____ | _____ |
| Signature | Date |

Come on, now! No school district anywhere in this country requires newly hired principals, or any other school administrator, to sign such a pledge. The mere thought of it is absurd! Or is this another list of those "less well-defined expectations" we looked at in Chapter 1? Perhaps we should take a closer look at what this hypothetical pledge states—maybe there's some important information to extract from this attention-getting device.

Hierarchical Lines of Authority

First, let's examine the statement that you "will accept the division of labor and responsibility." In any organization, the hierarchical lines of authority show up in a number of formats, that is, organizational charts, job descriptions, written contracts, policies, rules, regulations, procedures, and schedules. Each individual job description includes specific tasks and responsibilities. As a principal who expects to be effective in your job, you'll need to learn the right person to contact when you need assistance, not just the right department. You'll work hard to develop rapport with key personnel in every department at the district level, and you'll be careful not to encroach on others' assigned responsibilities and tasks. When you make contacts to complete tasks, as an effective principal you'll ensure that appropriate credit is given.

Figure 2.1. School District Organizational Chart

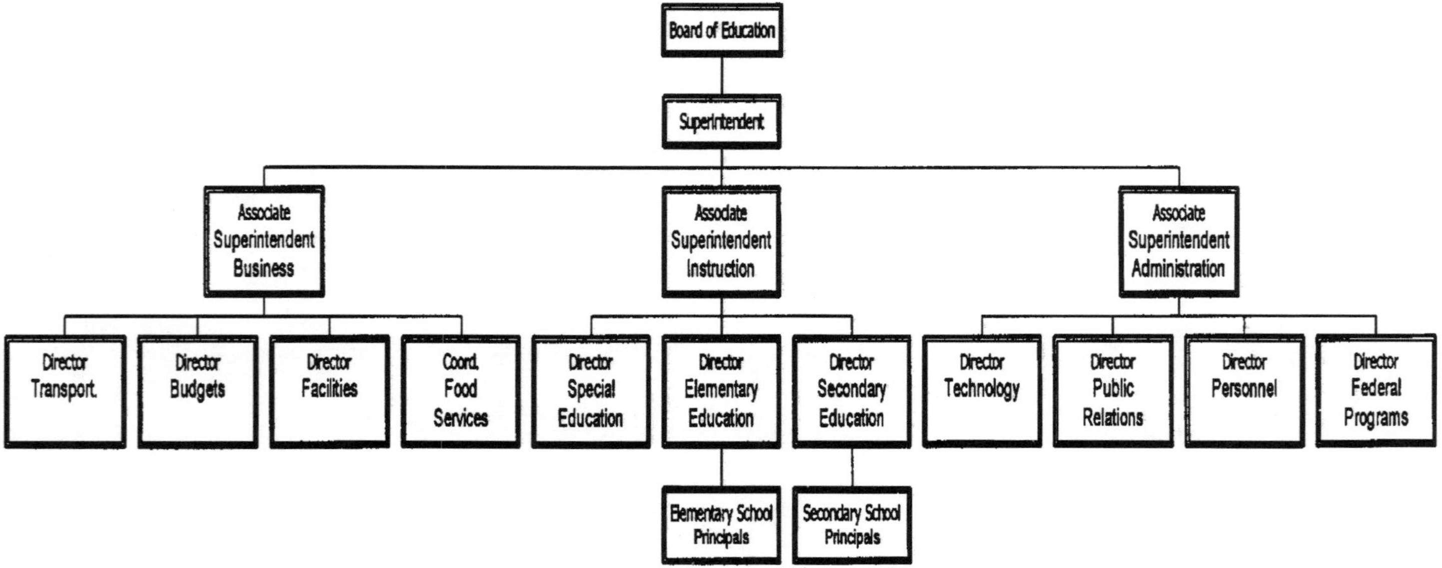

The Problem of Allegiance

The statement "make myself *subordinate* to the school district and its goals" is a difficult statement to explain and frequently opens the door to much discussion. You may have noted that Chapter 1 doesn't mention student welfare as a key rationale for selecting you for the principalship. Once you are chosen to be a principal, your primary allegiance is to the superintendent and the board of education. This may be a shift from what you felt was your primary focus and central allegiance as a teacher. If asked, as a teacher, you would most likely have responded, "My first allegiance is to my students; my second is to their parents."

But what if after being asked the first question, you were presented with a rejoinder such as this: "But you're employed by the school district. They sign your paycheck. You couldn't be a teacher in this school without a contract. Isn't your first allegiance really to your employer?" Now, you can hold out for the higher cause—the politically correct public relations response for all employees in a school system—which has to be, "The kids are our most important concern. Kids come first." Although kids are, in fact, your most important duty, as a principal you now represent the board of education. *You're caught in the middle.* You have been selected to represent the board as its emissary, an immediate superior to a faculty and staff. They teach and support the school. You supervise, evaluate, recommend new hires, and take an active role in due-processing ineffective members of the faculty and staff. You manage the building and are considered to be a community leader. Your duty continues to be directed to the welfare of children and their parents, but has now expanded to include faculty and staff. Your primary allegiance, then, is to the board. You can't fulfill your duty without such allegiance. You really are caught in the middle, aren't you? You may argue, "Okay, I can split my allegiance. I believe that I can equalize my allegiance across the spectrum: from kids to the board!" Good luck. Perhaps the following statement will help: Effective principals externalize their feelings of duty across the spectrum, but recognize the fact that their true allegiance is first and foremost, to themselves, their jobs, the board. Although they may not be able to publicize it, they know that they can't help teachers teach, kids learn, and parents survive without the platform of the principalship from which to direct. They want that platform and recognize that it's been provided for them exclusively by their employers. A principal's duty to kids, teachers, and parents can't be accomplished without allegiance to, and support from, superiors.

Organizational Decision Making

Okay, now that your allegiance is pointed in the right direction(s), let's examine the statement "participate in organizational decision making on a *rational* basis." At first glance, this may seem to be a "don't rock the boat" statement. But all institutions need some sort of structure to survive. Individuals in that structure must be willing to interact and behave in prescribed ways. "In order to survive, the elements of strength, faith in purpose, vigor, and cohesion must be built into or acquired by an organization" (Boles & Davenport, 1975, p. 66). Effective principals do their homework prior to attending districtwide meetings and participate in an intelligent, informed manner. When they suggest change, they provide justifiable evidence. When they debate, they do so in a nonabrasive way. And when group decisions are made, whether they agree or not, they implement those decisions without further discussion. They become a valued part of the district's administrative team.

Organizational Confidentiality

The statement "maintain organizational confidentiality" may sound like school districts have a cache of secrets they don't want disclosed. The question is, why wouldn't they? The board of education, superintendent's office, and districtwide administrators make certain key decisions each year that call for appropriate groundwork to be laid prior to public announcement. Matters concerning transferring or terminating personnel, changing school boundaries, closing buildings, or moving students from one building to another to equalize enrollment are just a few of the kinds of decisions that must be internally discussed and thoroughly planned before any public announcement is made. Principals are actively involved in this kind of planning and are expected to hold certain pieces of information in confidence until the board or superintendent is ready to release them to the community. Most of this confidence holding, or "secrecy," is the result of routine short- and long-range organizational planning. Occasionally, however, principals find themselves caught in a bind. A teacher or parent might ask, "I heard through the grapevine that the board is planning to close Sunnyside School. Any truth to this rumor?" Now, remember the discussion concerning allegiance? Here's a classic dilemma that might pit your personal values against your allegiance to your employer. You know that the board has made such a decision and will announce it in about 6 weeks. Is it okay to fib and say, "I haven't heard anything about that"? Is it okay to simply say, "Yes, but don't tell anyone that I told you"? Or how about a cop-out like, "I don't respond to rumors"? (Watch your public relations quotient plummet after that one!) Here we clearly need a bottom line. Someone needs to declare, "Sometimes you have to fib, it's okay—or whatever. Well, no one is going to give you a "bottom line" for this extremely common situation. So the dilemma—a potential clash between values and allegiance—is yours to deal with. It's the world of a principal!

Legitimate Right to Authority

How do you feel about the pledge to "submit to and legitimize authority"? You like your job as a school principal. You want to succeed and to keep that job. This doesn't mean that you can't debate or discuss your personal position on a matter with a superior. It simply means that when you're given a direct and lawful order, you will comply. You manage your faculty and staff and the students in your school the same way. Although you invite them to discuss matters of concern with you, you expect your faculty, staff, and students to recognize and respect your right to make decisions in the best interest of your school.

Cooperation With Peers

Consider the statement, "seek personal and professional satisfaction in cooperation with but never at the *expense* of peers." Now think about it in relation to this brief scenario. The assistant superintendent refuses to approve your plan for an extended student lunch period. He's aware that none of your fellow principals support your plan. They feel strongly that your plan would put pressure on them to do the same, and they believe that such a move would adversely affect their academic programs. So, you run to the superintendent hoping that she will overrule her assistant. That's called an end run in organizations. And although it is an often-repeated and respected play in football, it works only once in the school business. Your peers are your best friends as a principal. They make dangerous enemies.

Central Control

Finally, let's look at the statement, "*accept* centralized control of my actions and initiatives." For any school district to be successful, it must have structure. If we were studying the mores or folkways of our culture, we might run across this 1906 definition of structure: "a framework, or apparatus, or perhaps only a number of functionaries set to cooperate in prescribed ways at a certain conjunction" (Sumner, 1906, p. 53). Structure has long been recognized as a mainstay of organizational success. In any organization, including school districts, there has to be some form of structure or central control. The concept of centralized authority (control) is rooted in classical theory of management. At its core are beliefs such as

- Efficiency is the sole measure of productivity.
- Human behavior is rational.
- Work should be separated into units and closely supervised.
- Uniform policies, rules, and regulations are necessary to ensure proper control.
- Individuals are not inclined to work hard.
- A hierarchy of authority is necessary to establish organizational goals and to coordinate efforts toward their achievement. (Hanson, 1996)

Central control doesn't mean that one person or a small group of people completely run the show, but rather that appropriate authorities in the overall bureaucracy oversee the multiple and distinct parts of the organization to ensure that they are moving *simultaneously* toward common goals.

In studies specific to effective principals and effective schools, an interesting anomaly can be found. It's one that's seldom mentioned in the literature. Principals and other administrators in a typical school district who are considered to be "company people" or effective "team members" are able to develop a fairly high level of autonomy, albeit *directed autonomy*, in their positions. In other words, when superiors trust that a principal is willing to accept central control as a fact of doing business, there is a tendency not to micromanage that particular school and to leave nearly all decisions (actions and initiatives) in the hands of that principal. This earned trust from superiors is the situation you want to fashion for yourself and your school. Directed autonomy is an arrangement in which you and your faculty and staff are empowered, and even encouraged, to do things your own way (Waterman, 1987). But such empowerment is not without boundaries. You'll never have exclusive autonomy in the school business. Your role as a *semi-autonomous* principal will be discussed in detail in Chapter 4.

THE BOTTOM LINE

Although the hypothetical pledge at the beginning of this chapter is clearly offensive in today's society, it offers some truths. As a teacher, you played a certain role; you were part of a faculty culture. As a principal attempting to be effective, you have to leave that particular culture and move into another. You need to understand how the district-level administrative culture is different and recognize that the expectations it holds for you are also different. All school districts have some readily identifiable cultural characteristics in common: (a) they involve people, (b) the people interact, (c) interactions are usually ordered and prescribed, (d) interactions help to achieve some joint objectives and goals, and (e) objectives and goals need to be seen as personal expectations. These characteristics objectify organizational values, principles, and history as described below:

> There is a body of cultural values, relatively stable and universal, that illuminates the behavioral manifestations of all social effort and, in particular, the public provision of educational services.
>
> These cultural values may be called "principles." They are the frequently unverbalized basic arguments for taking this course or that, for behaving in this fashion or other, for a positive rather than a negative decision on a specific issue. The authors believe that those distillations of what people

think of as "goodness" in the management of public affairs are things that well up from the long history of man's learning to live and work side by side with his fellows. (Mort & Ross, 1957, p. 33)

The key elements that characterize an effective school district are unity of purpose and interdependence. The primary purpose (unity of purpose) of a school district is clear—provide for the education of the youth of the community. There are secondary purposes as well. In this chapter, however, we have been dealing mainly with interdependence—that is, a principalship is not a sovereign state. If your school district is to operate with unity of purpose and reach its primary and secondary goals, your district expects you, and all other administrators, to adopt its administrative culture—to play a role. This role demonstrates to your superiors that you are now a part of the total organization. You are no longer a faculty member, and it's up to you to learn, understand, and internalize the unique characteristics of your school system at the district level. It's your first step toward effectiveness as a principal.

REFERENCES

Boles, H. W., & Davenport, J. A. (1975). *Introduction to educational leadership.* New York: Harper & Row.

Hanson, E. M. (1996). *Educational administration and organizational behavior* (4th ed.). Boston: Allyn & Bacon.

Mort, P. R., & Ross, D. H. (1957). The humanitarian considerations in school administration. In *Principles of School Administration* (2nd ed., Chap. 3). New York: McGraw-Hill.

Sumner, W. G. (1906). *Folkways.* Boston: Ginn.

Waterman, R. H. (1987). *The renewal factor: How the best get and keep the competitive edge.* New York: Bantam.

3

One Size Doesn't Fit All

Matching Your Personality With the Role of Principal

ABOUT THIS CHAPTER

When you accept a job as principal, the board of education and the superintendent of schools give you a new identity. When you get to your assigned school, you'll probably park in a spot clearly marked "Principal." Your principal's set of keys will open your office door—a door clearly marked "Principal," and you can sign all school correspondence with the word "Principal" after your name. The local newspaper will announce your appointment by stating something like "So-and-so has been named 'Principal' at such-and-such school."

All this is great, and you should be proud of your title. Effective principals have a sense of identity that doesn't depend on title, perks, or status, but rather on their own personal values, however—values so integral to their natures that they can't be denied. Effective principals know where they came from, where they're going, and why they're going there (whence, whither, and why). When bosses, peers, and subordinates see them in this light, they describe their style as confident. When they follow through, they describe their style as authentic. Style—confidence and authenticity—is the substance of leadership. Sure, effective principals adapt to the administrative culture of their school districts and certainly demonstrate loyalty (allegiance) to immediate superiors, but they understand that the *position* of "Principal" is only a title that has little meaning, little authority, little authenticity without social interchange. Such interchange takes place when would-be followers grant would-be leaders *personal* authority.

REFLECTIVE POINT

Secondary Impression—The second step toward the aggregate
impression *of you that you want others to have*

When we work with people or encounter them on multiple occasions, over time we continue to modify our perceptions based on our observations of their behavior or actions in different circumstances. To the extent that those actions confirm our expectations, they reinforce our general impression (Chapter 1) and our primary impression (Chapter 2). To the extent that those actions contradict our expectations, we add the new impressions to our initial perception. We gain a better, fuller picture of who these people are and what we can expect from them in the future.

Our secondary impressions help us make decisions about whether we like a person, are comfortable in his or her presence, and would like to get to know him or her better. As you move from creating a primary impression to developing a positive secondary impression, there are some sociological pitfalls you need to consider, which this chapter examines.

THE COMPATIBILITY OF
PERSONAL ATTRIBUTES AND
THE PRINCIPAL'S ROLE: PITFALLS

Position Versus Personal Authority

In your role as "The Principal," you've been given the authority to manage or run your school. You've been given *position* authority. We've already briefly discussed the hierarchical lines of authority and noted that lines of authority show up in a number of formats, for example, organizational charts, job descriptions, contracts, and policies. We know that authority flows downward from the top (i.e., the superintendent and the board) through all the various levels of the school district. It works the same way in the school business as it does in any organization.

Now, let's examine the explicit authority that you've been given in the principalship. First, you've been given the authority (position) to manage your school. With that authority comes the right to—the right to do—to do—well, really nothing! Oh, you can order supplies, sign requisitions, rearrange the furniture in your office, and give instructions to subordinates—but position authority is really honorary, almost nonexistent, unless supplemented by *personal* authority. Your right to make decisions or to take actions that affect others is recognized as authentic by your subordinates only if they see your ability, not just your position, as credible and acceptable. Although position authority flows downward from superiors and gives you the right to *manage,* personal authority flows upward from followers and gives you the right to *lead.* Personal authority is essential for leaders. Principals who merely manage a school don't last long. You must be able to both manage and lead. And you must earn the right to lead, the power to lead, from your prospective followers.

So, what is personal authority? Research provides an interesting list of the personal factors that effective leaders possess (influential or authority) and the amount of effect aspiring leaders can deliberately have on such factors (Boles & Davenport, 1975, p. 408). We can paraphrase the list for the purpose of this discussion and omit those factors over which you have little or no influence (e.g., gender, race, height, etc.). As Table 3.1 indicates with a few examples, however, if you're going to be effective in your position, you can have some control in your quest for personal authority.

Although each factor is important and is incorporated throughout this book, one factor, *being visible,* deserves to be highlighted right from the start. For you to gain personal authority, your followers must have the opportunity to see and hear you in action. They must gain an impression of who you are, what you're going to do, and how you're going to address their personal and professional needs. Visibility is the key to others' aggregate impression of you as their potential leader, and it's the starting point for them to decide whether or not to give you the personal authority you need to do more than just manage them and their school. It's interesting to note that in recent years, months, and at times days, national groups (e.g., the National Policy Board, the Interstate School Leaders Licensure Consortium [ISLLC], state legislators, state boards of edu-

Table 3.1

How much control do leaders have regarding this factor?

	Factor	Not Much	Some	Much
		Amount of Control		
Having:	an engaging personality		X	
	an attractive physical appearance		X	
	a commanding voice (tone or quality)		X	
	organizational status		X	
	persuasive ability			X
	societal status		X	
Being:	able to manipulate others		X	
	admired			X
	identified with a cause		X	
	identified with a familiar figure		X	
	identified with the organization			X
	liked or loved			X
	respected		X	
	visible			X
Demonstrating:	ability or knowledge			X
	accomplishment			X
	commitment to a cause		X	
	commitment to the organization			X
	ethical standards			X
	responsibility		X	
	communication skills (diverse audiences)			X

cation, etc.) continue to add or subtract domains or categories to the factors listed above—all in an ongoing attempt to develop standards for the principalship. The problem of initial standards, measurable potential, and measurable accountability continues to be tossed back and forth among educators and policymakers.

Authenticity in Style and Its Relationship to Authority

There's a tendency to suggest that a person's style is neatly wrapped up in a package called *persona* or *charisma*. Some suggest that style is the manner in which you act, the way in which you outwardly manifest your personality. Still others focus on the importance of verbal communication, characteristic posture (i.e., ways of moving and gesturing), and so on. These multiple dimensions exist because the study of administrative style, like the overall study of leadership, is a multifaceted one, surrounded by a mass of myth, conventional wisdom, idealism, and illusion. Part of the reason for this confusion is that as a social science concept, the idea of leadership (style) evolves from the particular perspective one holds (Hanson, 1996). As a result, the concept of style, as an important attribute to any type of leadership role, has been the subject of hypothesis building for social scientists for years. Style, for lack of a better definition, is simply a characteristic way of behaving, and because nobody behaves in a characteristic fashion at all times and in all situations, the importance of style is questionable in the overall picture of authentic authority. When we examine personal authority in the light of style and one's ability to lead, however, one area seems to surface—authenticity.

The characteristics or attributes of being authentic consist of

- Being as fully aware as you can be (having as much information as possible about the situation and your role)
- Choosing alternatives to which to commit effort, devotion, and allegiance
- Taking responsibility for each choice, knowing that it may not be the optimum, while recognizing the imperfection of your awareness and the inherent risk
- Recognizing that good intentions are seldom an excuse (paraphrased from Bugental, 1965, p. 45)

When we compare these attributes with the characteristics of style, we find style defined as an intricate mix of personal philosophy, professional knowledge and experience, and situational variables.

Now, what do the preceding paragraphs really mean? In an earlier discussion, we said that principals must have (a) a strong sense of identity that doesn't rely on status, (b) values that are so central to their natures that they can't be denied, (c) knowledge of their cultural prejudices and the limitations that prejudices impose, and (d) an understanding of how far they can go in trying to be like others without compromising their own integrity. This synthesis is the essence of style. Effective principals know where they came from, where they're going, and why they're going there (again, whence, whither, and why). When bosses, peers, and subordinates see you in this light, they describe your style as confident. When you follow through, they describe your style as authentic. Style—confidence and authenticity—is the substance of leadership. How you develop professional and personal relationships with people, the kinds of expectations you set for others, and your ability to delegate authority will help to establish your style and your authenticity in the minds of others—another part of the aggregate impression of you that others will add to their "Reasons Why I Want to Follow That Person" file.

Now, you might ask, isn't there more that I need to know about style? You've given me the essence of style, but isn't this a bit narrow? And what about this persona or charisma thing?

Remember, the first paragraph said that the study of administrative style, like the overall study of leadership, is a multifaceted one, and the concept of leadership (style) evolves from the particular perspective one holds. Chapter 6 discusses the broader ramifications of style and the fact that the way we *perceive* people influences our *interpretation* of their behavior, thus, their style as we see it. The person perception process takes on considerable significance in the development of a person's perceived authenticity.

Arrogance Versus Confidence

Arrogance *n.* The state or quality of being arrogant. Arrogant *adj.* Overly convinced of one's own importance; overbearingly proud; haughty. Egotistical, self-admiring, presumptuous, conceited, overconfident, assuming. (*American Heritage Dictionary of the English Language*, 1970, p. 73)

Confidence *n.* Trust in a person or thing. A feeling of assurance or certainty, especially concerning oneself. Confident *adj.* Having assurance or certainty as of success. Having confidence in oneself, self-confident, self-assured, positive, optimistic, secure. (*American Heritage Dictionary of the English Language*, 1970, p. 279)

Using the definitions provided, see if you can definitively determine which of the statements in Table 3.2 demonstrate "arrogance" as opposed to "confidence." Let me help you a bit. Think: "eye of the beholder," "their perception," "how the message is received." Or "comparing me to you." Think also: Who is the person making the statement? What do I think of him or her? Would the statement seem arrogant coming from one particular person while from another it might demonstrate confidence? Now, try determining between arrogance and confidence in the following statements. Good luck!

Table 3.2

Statement	Arrogance	Confidence
There are no right answers in education, only best answers for each situation. Here's my best answer!		
No problem, boss, I've got everything under control.		
Give me a screwdriver, I can fix the damn thing.		
It's impossible to bring others up to the level of understanding that I have of the situation.		
Do, or do not. There is no try.[a]		
Your ignorance is encyclopedic.[b]		
I wasn't looking for a job when I came here; I won't be looking for one when I leave.		
I would have made a good Pope.[c]		
I can make a positive contribution to this effort.		
It would be easier if I just did it myself.		
Each problem that I solved became a rule which served afterwards to solve other problems.[d]		
I've always been the smartest person I know.		
How can I lose to such an idiot.[e]		
I never have to lie—I'm always right.		
It's easy to shine when you're surrounded by ignorance.		
My well-timed silence has more eloquence than most people's speech.		
The longer I live the more I see that I am never wrong about anything, and that all the pains I have so humbly taken to verify my notions have only wasted my time.[f]		
It is time I stepped aside for a less experienced and less able man.[g]		

a. Yoda, in the 1980 film *The Empire Strikes Back*.
b. Paraphrased from Abba Eban (1915-).
c. Richard Nixon (1913-1994).
d. René Descartes (1596-1650), *Discours de la méthode* (1637).
e. Shouted by the chess master Aaron Nimzovich (1886-1935).
f. George Bernard Shaw (1856-1950).
g. Attributed to Professor Scott Elledge on his retirement from Cornell University.

Now, did you really have enough information about the person who made each statement to make a judgment? Were they joking? Were these tongue-in-cheek kinds of remarks? Would different individuals or groups of people see these statements in the same light? You might want to check the citations, where given, for more information.

You were "the eye of the beholder" in this exercise. You were the principal interpreter. Remember, everything you say or do is interpreted by someone else's eye and ear. Be careful what you say and how you say it. Be cautious in your use of sarcasm. Although humor is an important part of any leader's repertoire, it should never be at someone's expense. I, of course, know this far better than you. I am clearly faultless!

Manipulation It Is—But Influence It Must Be Called

One of the most difficult issues in studying the principalship as a leadership role is the use of influence. Once you are in the role, influencing, routing, maneuvering, cajoling, *manipulating*, is a fine art. Most principals like to think of school leadership as a democratic process in which they, as professionals, oversee many competing forces in the formulation of ideas, policies, and procedures. In reality, things are not always so simple.

In fact, they rarely are. Here's the scoop.

You've been appointed to and are acting in the role of a highly trained professional, more knowledgeable about the field of education, education management, and leadership than most people, including your faculty and staff. Such knowledge should mean that you have information and skills that the average teacher or patron doesn't possess. The issue in the use of influence arises when you know that teachers or the public are making a poor choice from among limited alternatives. And the issue is this: At what point do you offer professional expertise that may not have been solicited, and when does the sharing of knowledge become a form of manipulation? An honest, effective leader will acknowledge that many of the tasks, the roles, the getting-things-done-or-resolved part of leadership constitute a degree of—yes, manipulation, that is, how a committee is formed, who you select to lead a group to a consensus, how you choose your words or phrases or body language in a faculty or parent meeting, the approach you choose to take in presenting a problem or an opportunity, how well you can debate all sides of an argument, and so on. There are many other tactical moves that effective leaders use to guide and change human situations from win-lose to win-win. Call them tactical, influential, whatever. They're all a kind of manipulation.

Clearly, to be a leader, you need a distinct concept of democratic principles and their use. You need a working understanding of how people think and react and what they value. But it makes an immense difference whether you consider yourself a controller of events by virtue of position or simply one more force or influence in a democratic arena. You're not being manipulative—you're simply leading people to the most effective conclusions. As the Taoist sage Lao-Tzu wrote in the 6th century B.C., "A leader is best when people barely know he [sic] exists. When our work is done, his [sic] aim is fulfilled, they will say, 'We did it ourselves'" (Heider, 1986, p. 159).

Proactivity and Foreseeability

Proactivity is based on the unique human endowment of self-awareness, according to Steven Covey (1989):

> The two additional unique human endowments that enable us to expand our proactivity and to exercise personal leadership in our lives are imagination and conscience. Through imagination, we can visualize the uncreated worlds of potential that lie within us. Through conscience, we can come in contact with universal laws or principles with our own singular talents and avenues of contribution, and with the personal guidelines within which we can most effectively develop them. Combined with self-awareness, these two endowments empower us to write our own script. Because we already live with many scripts that have been handed to us, the process of writing our own script is actually more a process of rescripting, or paradigm shifting. As we recognize the ineffective scripts . . . incorrect or incomplete paradigms . . . we can proactively begin to rescript ourselves. (p. 103)

Now, for a moment at least, let's leave our examination of the culture of schools and look at the culture of law. In a court of law, when a "reasonable standard of care" dispute arises between any two parties (in other words, when someone accuses you of doing something he or she thinks is wrong), the courts use the model of a "reasonable and prudent person" to help determine whether, in fact, you have. (Remember the definition of effective principal presented in the Introduction to this book?) This model portrays you as an abstract being who possesses the hypothetical ideals of human behavior that embody the community's ideals and assumes that you possess all the special skills and abilities of perfect person acting as a school principal (Dunklee & Shoop, 1993, pp. 57-58). This abstract being, to which you are compared, performs under the question of *foreseeability*. In other words, could you, should you, have foreseen or anticipated the results of your actions or inactions?

So, as Covey (1989) stated, "as we recognize [or foresee] the ineffective scripts . . . incorrect or incomplete paradigms . . . we can proactively begin to rescript ourselves" (p. 103). To be an effective principal, you must practice the fine art of foreseeing and rescripting. You must be able to foresee, to a high probability, what the consequences might be of decisions you are about to make, procedural positions you are about to assume, and tasks you are about to undertake and consequently to adjust your thinking and actions to fit desired outcomes.

We expect our leaders to be decisive and to act on problems without delay. At the same time, we expect effective conclusions. To be effective as a principal, you'll need to be able to rapidly plot and process a large number of "what ifs" prior to acting. How do you do that? Simply stated, you must continuously consider, seek to understand, and measure the parameters of the culture in which you work.

I'm So Busy I Don't Have Time to Think!

In the role of principal, you'll find little time for much *reflective* thinking. You'll be reflecting and thinking—all at the same time—while you're in action. What? Reflecting in action? Hmmm, let me think and reflect on that for a minute. Okay, I've reflected—but you'll find that most school-based situations that require your decision-making expertise don't allow time for reflective thinking. Why? Simply because they

- Are most often fluid, seldom linear, and therefore difficult to analyze

- Are subject to a number of interpretations, often conflicting
- Often don't seem to fit into a category you've ever seen before

And although you're expected to act quickly and decisively, the environment you'll be working in is, by its very nature, characterized by ambiguity and uncertainty, and no matter how hard you try to routinize things, a certain amount of disorder will continue to exist.

Understand that when we put X number of students in a building with Y number of adults, and continuously deal with Z number of parents and patrons, all kinds of new, interesting, and challenging "social events" arise. Does the word "happenstance" pop into your mind? Or maybe "fire fighting"? So, when will you have time to think? "Why is it that researchers report so few occasions in which 'administrators' are observed, as scientists frequently are, thinking reflectively—cogitating, mulling over a problem, considering alternatives in the dispassionate calm of a quiet retreat?" (Owens, 1998, p. 264).

Researchers tend to look for episodes that indicate that some kind of reflective thinking is taking place. And while they're still looking for reflection—presto!—definitive action has already taken place.

Researchers often fail to see that effective administrators' thought processes are inseparably woven into, and occur simultaneously with, action. They see the action—the end result—and wonder how that decision was made: When did reflective thinking take place? The answer: Effective principals reflect and think at the same time, most of the time. When principals walk the halls, visit classrooms, read, talk, supervise, and meet with others, all of these actions contain thought and reflection and, indeed, they are the ways in which principals do their thinking (Owens, 1998, p. 265).

So, you might ask, are you suggesting that effective principals are "mindless"? Not at all. "Connected ideas, which are the essence of thought, can be formed and managed outside the mind, with relatively little assistance from the mind" (Weick, 1983, p. 222). Again, we're seeing effectiveness in a principal's work as an "art," not a science (Schon, 1983, p. 240). Still confused? Think intuition! Intuition is a process by which the mind collects random bits of information, some without sensible intention, and then recalls bits and pieces when triggered by an event to formulate an answer to a prevailing question.[1] In other words, you've been formally trained and socialized to understand the culture you're working in. Right? Then you understand that although the culture is a complex one, you're able to see individual parts of the whole. You can also see, *intuitively*, the trees, not just the forest. And as a result, you can think and act quickly because the ramifications of your actions or inactions are already ingrained (socialized) in your mind as intuitive processes. As a result of your understanding of the culture you work in, you can easily break down a seemingly complex phenomenon into a relatively simple, quantifiable incident. To become an effective principal you must be able to think all the time, intertwining your thinking with your actions, and you must understand that you will seldom have time to sequence your thinking processes and action into specific steps. That's why effective principals often credit their success to a personal understanding of the culture in which they work, along with a whole lot of what they call "smart guessing," a.k.a. intuitive thinking.

Smart Guessing—Science or Art?

When you deal in the physical sciences, you know that many answers can be definitive because you have the advantage of time— time to gather information, develop a hypothesis, set up the situation, and test the hypothesis before you answer a question or make a decision. That's physical science methodology in action. If you were asked, "How long does it take a 2,000-pound hippopotamus to run 500 yards?" think about all the missing information you would need to have to give an accurate answer. You'd probably need to know the age of the hippopotamus, ground and terrain conditions, and the motivation of the animal (i.e., angry, lovelorn, hungry, protecting territory, etc.). You could answer this question through the application of common scientific testing, and you'd have the answer— maybe—in a week or so.

In the social science world of the principal, you'll frequently need to make decisions when full information doesn't exist or is not readily at hand. But the problem needs to be resolved now. Without fabricating, you can apply common sense, intuition, and even creativity to resolve the issue. In the social sciences, there's seldom a right answer, and in the principalship seldom the time, personnel, or money to fully research all of your decisions in advance. Your best guess will often be the best you can do. Each social science problem, when viewed through your own personal experiences and common sense, your own knowledge of the culture in which you work, with you using your ability to break down the question to its simplest elements, should give you the insight to quickly give a best answer based on smart guessing. Guesswork is more accurate than you may think. The law of averages will help you a lot—assuming you are using common sense to start with. At any point, your assumptions may be right or wrong, but because of the law of averages, goofs will frequently balance out. And whether you're right, near right, or dead wrong, you'll pick up positive marks from your subordinates for decisiveness.

The Nobel Prize-winning physicist Enrico Fermi used problems like the hippopotamus scenario to teach his students how to think for themselves. A typical Fermi problem doesn't contain all the information you need to solve the problem or answer the question with precision. Fermi recommended that you break problems and questions down to more manageable bits and then have the courage to make guesstimates and build simple assumptions based on your own ability to smart-guess. Effective principals do just that. When major issues aren't at stake, they trust their abilities enough to practice the art of quick smart guessing. By the way, it would take an average hippo, being of average mind, running on average terrain, 43 seconds to run 500 yards. Now, while you try to figure out the smart guessing that might lead one to this conclusion, teacher Pomeroy wants to know whether she can take her first-, second-, and third-year German classes outside today. She claims it's stuffy in her classroom. Hmmm, what time of day do those classes meet? What's the weather forecast? Is there a high or low probability of one or more of her students being stung by a bee or infected by a tick? Why is her room stuffy? Why don't you tell her you'll think about it and get back to her? By doing that, you'll have time to apply scientific methodology to her question. On the other hand—just go ahead and say yes. Risk is your middle name, isn't it?

THE BOTTOM LINE

Leaders lead by influencing others, and although you've been given the authority to manage or run your school, you possess only *position* authority. Your right to make decisions or to take actions that affect others is recognized as authentic by subordinates only if they see your ability, not just your authority, as credible and acceptable. You need to gain *personal* authority and earn the right to lead from your prospective followers. Personal authority is essential for leaders. Style—confidence and authenticity—is the substance of personal authority. Arrogance is never acceptable; confidence, however, is expected.

Influencing effective outcomes, by using the ability to foresee effective outcomes and to be proactive and intuitive in decision making and the capacity to think on your feet, involves exercising the *artistic ability* you'll need to employ and demonstrate in the day-to-day operations of your school. This artistic ability is enhanced by your personal knowledge of the culture in which you work.

As noted before, principals who merely manage a school don't last long. You must be able to both manage and lead. Being adept at managing assets does not make you a leader; it makes you a manager. "Management is doing things right; leadership is doing the right things. . . . Management is efficiency in climbing the ladder of success; leadership determines whether the ladder is leaning against the right wall" (Drucker & Bennis, cited in Covey, 1989, p. 101). Although one function of an effective principal is effective management (easily *gained* through position authority), effective principals must be able to lead people (not so easily *earned* through personal authority).

The relationship between effective principals and their followers is not one of merely power or position authority, but is a genuine sharing of mutual goals, needs, aspirations, and to some extent values. It is through this sharing that your personal authority emerges—the authority to do more than merely manage.

In the next chapter, we'll look at the organization and culture of a school and continue the process of understanding the developmental processes of personal authority and aggregate impression.

NOTE

1. Author's definition.

REFERENCES

American Heritage dictionary of the English language. (1970). (W. Morris, Ed.). Boston: American Heritage Pub. Co. & Houghton Mifflin.

Boles, H. W., & Davenport, J. A. (1975). *Introduction to educational leadership.* New York: Harper & Row.

Bugental, J. F. T. (1965). *The search for authenticity.* New York: Holt, Rinehart & Winston.

Covey, S. R. (1989). *The seven habits of highly effective people.* New York: Simon & Schuster.

Dunklee, D. R., & Shoop, R. J. (1993). *A primer for school risk management.* Boston: Allyn & Bacon.

Hanson, M. E. (1996). *Educational administration and organizational behavior* (4th ed.). Boston: Allyn & Bacon.

Heider, J. (1986). *Tao of leadership: Lao-Tzu's tao te ching adapted for a new age.* Atlanta, GA: Humanics Publishing Group.

Owens, R. G. (1998). *Organizational behavior in education* (6th ed.). Boston: Allyn & Bacon.

Schon, D. A. (1983). *The reflective practitioner: How professionals think in action.* New York: Basic Books.

Weick, K. E. (1983). Managerial thought in the context of action. In S. Srivastava (Ed.), *The executive mind.* San Francisco: Jossey-Bass.

4

Getting an "A"
in Ambiguity

Successfully Navigating the
Complexity of School Culture

ABOUT THIS CHAPTER

Schools are alive with distinct, stimulating, and often unpredictable events each day. When you're asked, "What's it like to be a principal—really, what goes on behind the scenes?"your best answer might be to simply respond, "Oh, I—I keep busy!" But if you want to give an answer that leaves the questioners with a more descriptive, albeit rather academic, picture, you might want to memorize the next two paragraphs, put them in your own words, and be prepared to explain what your job is in more succinct terms. In a nutshell, it's what this chapter is all about.

According to a team of researchers from the University of Illinois at Chicago, principals live in a world that's been described as "fluid," and here's why. In a typical school,

> actors on the political stage are constantly changing, contradictions abound, and solutions to problems often do not last. One group of parents may oppose another. Factions may develop among the school staff, and some of these will ally with outside groups. Even the controls exercised by the

organizational hierarchy may change as chief officers come and go. The rules of the managerial game will be altered by the decisions of federal bureaucrats, the whims of the state legislature or the judiciary, and the initiatives of local politicians. The pressures that force a change in policy from above may be met by an equally powerful counterforce from staff members and parents below. To bow to one is to alienate the other; to compromise by bending a rule may alienate both. (Morris, Crowson, Porter-Gehrie, & Hurwitz, 1984, p. 223)

A principal's professional life balances precariously in the middle of a tug-of-war between competing interests and multiple constituencies. To be effective, you have to develop a high tolerance for ambiguity and learn to function effectively where power is limited and the direction of the educational system is often unclear. The ability to survive, much less lead, hinges on your being able to successfully integrate special interests and multiple constituencies into a working unit.

Now, although the preceding two paragraphs might not provide the best answer to give your friends, they do partially represent the right answer. And although it's not important for your friends to fully understand your job, it is important for you to understand that the principalship is a complicated, and often ambiguous, role—more complicated, ambiguous, and "behind the scenes" than you probably were able to observe in your preprincipal position. Perhaps this chapter will provide some insight into why a principal might declare,

> There's politics around every corner. We'll make decisions at the school, but if a certain group of parents don't like them, all of a sudden there's a barrage of letters and phone calls and a decision floats down from above contrary to everything that was worked out at the school level. (A school administrator, cited in Walsh, 1998, p. C5)

And at the same time, a teacher might agree with the above and add,

> Today a school principal has to be more "the principal politician" than what he or she was intended to be—"the principal teacher," based on the British concept of the headmaster.

Constantly dodging bullets and having to placate this and that individual or group, a principal has less time to be an instructional leader. (A school administrator, cited in Walsh, 1998, p. C5)

REFLECTIVE POINT

Tertiary Impression—The third step toward the aggregate impression of you that you want others to have

Our third-level impressions are closely tied to our personal value systems and are key to our decisions to trust, make a commitment to, or follow another person. We form these tertiary impressions when we observe a person's behaviors toward others we care about or actions in situations that are value laden for us or in which we have a vested interest. To the extent that the person shares our value system and acts or behaves in a manner of which we approve, our impression of that person is enhanced. To the extent that we detect a divergent value system in the person or are disappointed in the person's behavior or actions, our impression of that person becomes more negative. It's important to keep this part of the aggregate impression you're attempting to build on and enrich as you move into Chapter 4.

THE MIDDLE MANAGEMENT CULTURE AND THE ACCOUNTABILITY SUBCULTURE

Multiple Constituencies

Let's take a closer look at those multiple constituencies that were mentioned previously. Remember the statement, "The ability to survive, much less lead, hinges on my being able to successfully integrate special interests and multiple constituencies into a working unit." We'll start by focusing on those multiple constituencies (sometimes referred to as *subcultures*) in the school and then on the basic dichotomy between various constituent or subculture needs and your ability to meet those needs.

When we look at the multiple constituencies, it's apparent that, first, there's a clear distinction between the roles of student and teacher:

- *Students* are compelled to enter school in the mandatory role of student and are inducted into adult life through activities not necessarily relevant to their immediate interests. Their primary interest is not necessarily an orderly learning environment.

- *Teachers* voluntarily enter their roles and receive continuing incentives in return for their professional contributions. They tend to be very interested in an orderly working and teaching environment.

Second, there's a clear distinction between the roles of support staff and those of students and teachers:

- *Secretaries, clerks, and maintenance workers* voluntarily enter their roles and although their institutional tasks further the education program, they may be more concerned with working conditions and job security than with the support of an orderly teaching and learning environment.

- *Guidance counselors, program coordinators, librarians, and department heads* voluntarily enter their roles and although their institutional tasks further the education program, they often see themselves in a semimanagerial role that can, and often does, conflict with the role of the classroom teacher.

- *Assistant principals* are appointed and voluntarily assume their roles. Although their tasks further the education program, they often find that rather than making administrative or policy decisions, they're responsible for implementing decisions made by the principal. Although their primary interest usually focuses on making a difference that will cause the principal to recommend a promotion, their responsibilities are myriad and subject to the immediate and extremely varied needs of the principal.

Third, there's a clear distinction between the roles of central office administrators; board of education members who represent the community at large; and school-based teachers, students, and support staff:

- *Central office administrators* are appointed and voluntarily assume their roles. We need to look at central administration in two ways—line and staff. *Line administrators* include the superintendent, associate or assistant superintendents, and others who report directly to the superintendent. Their main responsibilities are *directing, controlling, monitoring,* and *evaluating* the behavior of people and *designating* preferred outcomes for programs in the organization. They maintain firm hierarchical control of authority in their respective roles as examiners and evaluators. They establish and maintain vertical communications and develop written policies, rules, regulations, and procedures to establish standards and guide actions. To meet the immediate needs of the district, they add staff positions, supervisory and administrative, to the hierarchy of the organization as necessary to meet problems that arise from changing conditions encountered by the organization. *Staff administrators* usually report to an assistant superintendent, and their main responsibilities are *coordinating* the behavior of people and *implementing* programs to achieve preferred outcomes. As school districts expand in size (population, programs, etc.), staff positions such as chairperson, director, and coordinator often appear. As programs, either mandated or elective, appear or become more complex, additional positions start to appear (e.g., specialists, directors of districtwide activities, coordinators of special programs, etc.). The larger the district, the more complex the bureaucracy becomes.
- *Board of education members* are elected or otherwise selected by the community at large and are the legal authority for the community's public schools. The society they represent "demands allegiance to certain values and enforces constitutional safeguards. Society's values—freedom of speech, a tolerance of ethnic and religious differences, equal treatment, a right to learn—take precedence over local narrow-mindedness" (Morris et al., 1984, p. 224).

Fourth, there's a clear distinction between the school, the school district, and the patrons in an individual school's community:

- *The local community* voices the aspirations of parents for their children, as well as the neighborhood's interest in maintaining good schools, qualified teachers, and a livable environment. Teachers and other staff members have a tradition of professional autonomy and standards. The principal usually shares the teachers' views of the importance of instruction and the value of independence.

And then, there's you:

- *The principal* sits at the center of this world of subcultures. As principal, you'll have the responsibility to meld these disparate interests into a working unit, attending simultaneously to both individual and institutional needs. As principal, you'll have to respond to the wishes and demands of a sometimes-bewildering array of masters. Both line and staff administrators often see themselves as being on the front line, whereas principals often see themselves as being on the firing line. Teachers see themselves as being on both the front and firing lines. Without effective management by line administrators, there is often disagreement between staff administrators and building principals as to who has final authority in determining what's right for individual schools. You're responsible for countering the continuous influences of divisiveness and diversity.

For you to be an effective principal, your first responsibility is to manage the unpredictability—the culture—of the school community. "Community" is defined by three key areas in which a principal must balance school improvement with stability and control—all in support of a quality education for students: (a) student discipline and control, (b) parent and community involvement, and (c) teacher and staff performance. You must manage both stabilization and improvement initiatives to harmoniously unite multiple constituencies in an effective school. Effective principals recognize that a high degree of tension exists between such initiatives, however. Too much stabilization will deaden the enterprise; too much improvement can be disorienting and counterproductive.

There are other constituencies to which you must answer as well. These include local business owners, neighborhood churches, local civic groups and clubs. Among the expectations introduced in Chapters 1, 2, and 3, two major expectations were implied: (a) you will effectively *manage* the school's environment, ensuring a controlled setting for teaching and learning; and (b) you will provide *leadership* for students, faculty, and staff, empowering them to focus on excellence in their individual roles. So, we now know that part of these expectations is to be able to manage and lead multiple constituencies.

In an early sociological explanation of life in schools, one researcher noted that the world of the local school is a social world, a "tangled web of interrelationships" between human beings "who have much in common but are also in conflict." Teachers, administrators, pupils, and parents relate to one another in the confined setting of the school quite often as "antagonistic forces" existing in a state of "perilous equilibrium" (Waller, 1965, pp. 1-14).

To be an effective principal, you'll need to quickly learn to adapt and respond to multiple constituencies. Accordingly, perhaps your most important role is to manage and resolve conflict. But, to which of your constituencies do you owe primary allegiance?

Experienced, effective principals have all successfully faced the loyalty dilemma inherent in dealing with multiple constituencies, each of which want primary allegiance. The fundamental question first introduced in Chapter 2—*to whom does the principal owe his or her greatest loyalty?*— continues to evade a simple answer. Many researchers have asked basically the same question: Which of the many categories of constituents is the principal's primary reference group when each group has a legitimate claim on the principal? How do effective principals resolve this issue? Many researchers have described the problem, but none has developed a definitive answer. We do know that effective principals balance the needs and desires of all the groups they serve with, for, and under. They balance their loyalties in such a way that no group feels unimportant or left out. We also know that principals working in turbulent or multiconstituent relationships experience a feeling of relative isolation (Blumberg & Greenfield, 1980, p. 233). Leadership *is* lonely.

One researcher noted,

> More than anything else, the principal needs to learn how to keep the school functioning while he [sic] learns how he [sic] can move the many stakeholders [constituencies] in the school towards complementary visions of success. The job is never finished and the principal is never completely successful; but somehow the principal must do the equivalent of adjusting the engine of a powerful racing car while it is circling the track at 200 miles per hour. He [sic] dare not over-adjust, and the car must be kept on course. (Donaldson, 1991, cited in Erlandson, 1994, p. 4)

Just think—with all these constituencies surrounding you, demanding your allegiance and attention to their particular needs, you can rest assured that life as an effective principal is never dull.

The Importance of Identifying an Effective Mentor

You must learn from the mistakes of others. You can't possibly live long enough to make them all yourself.

—Sam Levenson

We discussed the importance of catching the eye of a mentor prior to becoming a principal in Chapter 1. The significance of a supportive mentor doesn't end at the point of promotion to the principalship, however. Although you will certainly inherit a complete set of rules, regulations, policies, and procedures, you won't find most of the answers to your everyday problems in such tomes. Now, you'll need someone to help you fill in the blanks, the missing parts, and the expectations so carefully left out of the "great books." In addition, now, more than ever, you'll need someone already in the principalship you can trust, who'll hold your questions and comments in confidence and provide a sounding board for your decision-making dilemmas.

A group of New York City principals identified a wide range of skills, processes, and information learned from on-the-job mentors. Some of these included:

- Strategies to help with decision making
- Ideas to develop communications
- Guidance in building relationships with constituencies
- Recognition of the reality that change takes time
- Acceptance of the fact that the principal's job is often reactive rather than proactive
- Basics of crisis management and litigation avoidance
- Ways to delegate tasks and tips on scheduling, organization, and time management
- Ways to develop and maintain a strong network of colleagues
- Insider information regarding daily or standard operating procedures not found in manuals or regulations
- Assistance in interpreting the contract
- The necessity to be assertive in actions and confident in decisions
- Direction, comfort, focus, and ways to enjoy and rise above the challenges of the job (Cited in Erlandson, 1994, p. 5)

Research tells us that beginning principals, on their way to becoming effective, typically progress along a similar developmental continuum (Hall & Parkay, 1992). For example, they see the following as immediate priorities—each of which can be strengthened by a supportive relationship with a mentor. Mentors can be invaluable resources when you want to

- Emphasize visibility and communication
- Develop an administrative team
- Organize administrative procedures and budgetary processes
- Study established policies and procedures

In addition, beginning principals benefit from tapping the knowledge and practical experience of their mentors as they actively seek resolution to the following common roadblocks to early success:

- Survival (New principal experiences the shock of beginning leadership, concern with sorting things out.)
- Control (New principal's primary concern is setting priorities and getting on top of the situation.)
- Stability (New principal's frustrations become routinized; management-related tasks are handled effectively and efficiently.)
- Professional actualization (New principal's confirmation comes from within; focus is on attaining personal vision.)

And finally, a skillful mentor can help inexperienced principals develop

- A clear, informed vision of what they want their schools to become
- An effective translation of this vision into clear goals and expectations for students, teachers, and administrators
- A school climate that supports the attainment of these goals and expectations (Rutherford, 1985)

The importance of a mentor to help you get your feet firmly planted can hardly be overemphasized. Without some assistance, you may place undue emphasis on trivial events or you may become bogged down by inordinate concentration on two obvious challenges that characterize and can impede the adjustment stage of a beginning principal—the challenges of dealing with multiple tasks and communicating with various audiences.

There is no clear course for you to follow other than what has taken place in the school before you were named principal. If the school was an effective one in the immediate past, chances are that your predecessor's shoes may be too big for you to immediately fill. If the school was ineffective, your shoe size won't matter, as you won't have any shoes to fill. A mentor can provide you with shoes that fit, a simple road map to follow, and assistance in identifying a clear course regardless of whether your appointment is to an effective school or to an ineffective one.

"Would you tell me, please, which way I ought to go from here?" asked Alice.

"That depends a good deal on where you want to get to," said the cat.

"I don't much care where," said Alice.

"Then it doesn't much matter which way you go," said the cat.

"So long as I get somewhere," Alice added as an explanation. (Carroll, 1992, p. 89)

If, like Alice, you don't care where you really want to go, then it doesn't matter what direction you take. If, however, you want to be effective in your efforts as principal—if you want to get started in the right direction and stay on track—then a skillful mentor (Cheshire Cat) can help you set personal priorities and assist you in plotting a path that can guide you to success, rather than just to "somewhere."

Formal and Informal Authority Structures: Factors to Consider

Weber's (1910/1964) concept of rationality (or authority) in organizations like school districts is illustrated in his taxonomy of domination.

The taxonomy describes three types of authority—charismatic, traditional, and legal. Charismatic authority, power based on the charismatic attraction of a leader that results in an emotional follower-leader relationship, will be examined in Chapter 6. Traditional power, power based on dominance inherent to a position (i.e., the position itself legitimizes certain authority and accompanying privileges that can be exercised by the position holder), was discussed in Chapter 2 and will be reexamined in Chapter 6. Legal power is based on a body of principles, rules, and laws that provide the authority for the position. Weber considered legal power to be best for forming the foundation of an ideal bureaucratic organization.

It's imperative that all educators, especially those in managerial or leadership positions, have a working knowledge of their obligations under the laws affecting schools and the education process, but this is not a school law book. Here, we need to examine those influences on authority that are not commonly mentioned in a school law book, but have a substantial impact on the day-to-day operations, including the thinking and action processes of an effective principal.

And because this book is primarily directed toward the study of the culture of education administration, it's imperative that we examine how policy and the regulations that support policy are made.

The term *regulation* has several meanings. From a strictly legal perspective, the word is often used to describe nonconstitutional and nonstatutory rules promulgated by public departments, agencies, or bureaus (Imber & Van Geel, 1993). In school districts, regulations commonly refer to administrative directives developed by the superintendent and staff to support policy mandated by the school board. Unlike policy statements, however, regulations are not formally adopted by the board and usually fall somewhere in the following categories:

- *Mandatory:* Regulations designed to accomplish absolute consistency in implementation with an emphasis on prescribing action, not on encouraging administrative thinking. (Thou shalt . . .)
- *Directory:* Regulations that suggest certain actions, but typically allow some administrative discretion in application, to account for the idiosyncrasies of individual schools. (In general, thou shalt . . .)
- *Discretionary:* Regulations that permit wide discretion on the part of the administrator (principal). (Thou shalt use common sense and expertise . . .)
- *Proscriptive:* Regulations that merely inform the administrator of prohibited actions or specify which selected personnel may take action. (Thou shalt not . . .) (Clemmer, 1991, cited in Kowalski, 1999)

Now, there's a coequal pair of bottom lines in this examination of authority factors. Here's the first. As a school principal, you want as much earned authority as possible so your superiors will allow you as much discretionary power as you need to make the kinds of decisions necessary to ensure that your school becomes and remains effective. Hey, that's easy. You'll just do a good job and they'll give it to you. But there's the second bottom line you'll need to understand. Where does discretionary power really come from and what do you really need to understand to gain such power? Remember, we're now examining nonconstitutional and nonstatutory authority, or power.

We all recognize the fact that the system of governance of elementary and secondary education involves a complex, dynamic, often confusing and contentious division of authority among federal, state, and local governments. The legal structure is only a part of the real system of governance, however. So, here's your introduction to the second bottom line.

Numerous factors affect and influence educational authority and decision making without actually having any real legal authority to do so. These include (and the list here is far from complete) such groups as

- The National Education Association and other associations and unions
- Professional associations grouped around various subjects taught in schools
- Trade publications
- Legal action groups such as the National Association for the Advancement of Colored People (NAACP) and the American Civil Liberties Union (ACLU) that influence education policy by promoting or assisting in key litigation
- Parents groups such as the Parent-Teacher Association (PTA) that are active lobbyists for their education concerns
- Agencies and companies that prepare standardized tests such as the Educational Testing Service, which by virtue of the widespread use of its standardized tests, monitors and reports the so-called conditions of our districts, by state, and nationwide

So, your second bottom line is this: The effective principal continuously monitors the efforts and the agendas of special interest organizations. Effective principals understand that local, regional, and national groups have a substantial impact on the administration of education, even though they are not part of its formal authority structure.

If you're an effective principal, and if your school consistently demonstrates success in the education process under your leadership, then you should earn the authority to make the kinds of discretionary decisions that keep you and your school just that—effective.

But with so many outside influences, can the bureaucracy allow this to happen? Do your superiors trust you enough to give you free rein?

> Trainers shackle young elephants with heavy chains to deeply embedded stakes. In that way the elephant learns to stay in its place. Older elephants never try to leave even though they have the strength to pull the stake and move beyond. Their conditioning limits their movements with only a small metal bracelet around their foot-attached to nothing. (Belasco, 1990, p. 2)

Effective principals are able to convince their community, their superiors, and the board of education that although the board has the right and the ultimate authority to make decisions, it's entirely possible that education professionals like themselves and their faculties can make the best decisions in their schools. We hope so. After all, effective principals and effective faculties are not elephants or even the monkeys that were described in the Introduction to this book

There is no contradiction here. The board has the legitimate or formal authority. Effective principals just want them to delegate the right to act responsibly—within the laws, rules, regulations, policies, and procedures—and allow them the space, the freedom, to do their job. Remember, at the beginning of this chapter we noted that as a principal you will be responding to multiple rather than simple constituencies, that it's imperative that you view the school setting as a political arena, and that managerial decisions must be negotiated amid many competing interests (Wiles, Wiles, & Bondi, 1980). You must now add informal authority structure to your menu of multiple constituencies. It's dangerous to assume that the organizational world, a world now far different from when Weber first published his taxonomy, possesses bureaucratic harmony, with the political problems of policy making solved. Today, effective principals have to possess a high tolerance for ambiguity and quickly learn to function effectively where power is limited and the direction of the educational system unclear (Blumberg & Greenfield, 1980).

If you want to find out how an informal structure can quickly change to formal and how many informal groups are out there, simply write an editorial for your local newspaper. I suggest you title it: "Back Off, You Laypeople, Let Us Professionals Run *Our* Schools." You'll get a lot of response. You've aggravated the perpetual tension between legal authority and informal authority. You will have *dared* to suggest that the real expertise lies with professional educators. Is your résumé up to date?

Theory Frequently Drowns in the Fishbowl

In Chapter 1, we looked at the fishbowl atmosphere common to the culture of administration. Now, we're talking about the culture of a typical school. Let's take a look at the kind of fishbowl you'll encounter in your typical school. Let's assume the question is, can you train all the fish in the bowl to consistently circle in the same direction? To answer this question, we need to examine a phenomenon commonly found in the culture of a typical school: the interesting interaction between theory (fish can be trained to circle in the same direction) and practice (fish are naturally in perpetual chaos, so live with it and train yourself to adjust). The management/administrative theories we read about and discuss in relationship to the education process are not without value. Effective principals learn how to use theory to their best advantage, however. They know that although theory has its merits, it also has limitations, and it's extremely important to know and understand the difference.

First, let's examine what we'll call traditional management/administrative theory, and second, let's look at its relationship to typical effective schools. Traditional management/administrative theory has merit when applied to situations of practice that

- Are characterized by *linear* conditions
- Are, or can be, *tightly* structured without adverse effects
- Lend themselves to a *routine level of competence and performance*

Traditional management/administrative theory has limitations when applied to situations of practice that

- Are characterized by *nonlinear* conditions
- Are, by the nature of the organization, *loosely* structured

Table 4.1

List A	as opposed to	List B
Discrete goals		Multiple and competing goals
Easily measured outcomes		Difficult-to-measure outcomes
Single solutions to problems		Multiple and competing solutions
Structured tasks		Unstructured tasks
Steady, predictable environment		Dynamic environment
Tight management connections		Loose management connections
Indisputable operating procedures		Ill-defined operating procedures
Certain consequences of action		Indeterminate consequences of action
Clear lines of authority		Unclear and competing lines of authority

- Are designed to bring about *effectiveness* and an *extraordinary commitment to performance*

Which list in Table 4.1, List A or List B, most closely describes a typical school?

If you chose List A, either close the book now or go back and review it from the beginning. But don't drop out completely. You are partly right. If you chose List B, move ahead, but listen carefully; there's some crossover. Under List A, explicitness, clarity, pattern, and predictability are inherent. Administrative *tasks* can often be described as linear actions—for example, purchasing, submitting work orders, and developing bus routes. These are activities in which interactions with other people are simple, incremental, or nonexistent. In a school setting, however these tasks can quickly turn nonlinear and would appear under List B. Take for example an argument with the district's purchasing agent over which brand of equipment to buy; a work order that you believe is urgent for safety reasons that gets placed at the bottom of the pile by the district supervisor of maintenance; and oh, yes—an out-of-the-blue ice storm that wreaks havoc with your bus arrival or departure schedule. Is that the fire alarm I hear? What do you mean the cafeteria ran out of food? There are not enough substitute teachers available today?

The majority of human interactions that take place in a school are nonlinear. "Nonlinearity means that the act of playing the game has a way of changing the rules" (Gleick, 1988, p. 24). Let's imagine for a moment placing our canoe (you have one, don't you?) in our hypothetical fishbowl. If all the fish have been trained to swim in the same direction, the water will be moving along fairly smoothly. If, however, the fish are in perpetual training—in other words, they can't be fully trained—then you can anticipate some whitewater.

> Most managers are taught to think of themselves as paddling their canoes on calm, still lakes. They are led to believe that they should be pretty much able to go where they want, when they want, using means that are under their control. . . . But it has been my experience that you never get out of the rapids! . . . There are lots of changes going on at once. The feeling is one of continuous upset and chaos. (Vaill, 1989, p. 2)

Effective principals learn how to routinize situations as rapidly as possible. Some theorists call this routinization "situational management"; others point out that rather than discrete goal attainment, effective principals practice "pattern rationality." No matter what theoretical label you attach to the *non*linear events that make up the bulk of a principal's working environment, effective practice requires quick thinking that enables you to constantly test what is happening against what you know. Effective principals continuously think, practice, and act in linear ways regardless of the situations surrounding them.

So, a typical school must be viewed under both a linear and a nonlinear light. The difference, however, can be the same difference you would experience reading this entry under a 25-watt standard light bulb as compared to a 5,000-watt strobe light at a rock concert. What? The ceiling in Room 215 is falling and you can't have classes in that room today? Do I smell smoke? What do you mean managing a school is like tattooing soap bubbles?

The Importance of Climate

The concepts of organizational climate and culture are often used interchangeably, and some theorists regard them as overlapping. Although organizational climate represents the atmosphere in a school or school district that generates perceptions of expectations for work-related behavior, organizational culture is rooted in sociology and anthropology. In other words, climate focuses on the emotional message a school or school district sends, and culture deals with what a school or school district is (see Miskel & Ogawa, 1988; Owens, 1998).

Confused? Try this. Culture represents the symbolic nature of a school or school district-values, beliefs, and norms that are characteristic of the people in the school community; beliefs and values held in common by employees, patrons, and current and former students. Over time, these people with their distinct perspectives and contributions create the tapestry that represents the culture of their schools in a particular community. Although culture is the foundation of such a tapestry, it's only one of a number of environmental factors contributing to a school's or school district's climate.

The complete climate paradigm includes these environmental factors:

- The physical and material aspects of a school or district, described as its *ecology* (i.e., school buildings, equipment, technology, etc.)

- The people who represent the school or district, its *cast of characters* (i.e., administrators, teachers, students, patrons, other employees), and their needs, wants, motivations, and dispositions

- The organizational nature of the school or district—the *social system* (i.e., relationships between line and staff, grade organization, how conflict is addressed, how calendars and schedules are built, etc.) (Taguiri, 1968)

So, in short, "Culture refers to the behavioral norms, assumptions, and beliefs of an organization, whereas, climate refers to perceptions of persons that reflect these norms, assumptions, and beliefs" (Owens, 1998, p. 165).

Still confused? Let's get emotional. Think about how you feel when you walk into a school for the first time. There's a degree of truth to the common notion that visitors to a school building form first and important impressions based on what they see and feel and how they are treated. If the environment is warm and colorful and people are friendly and helpful, visitors' perceptions are more likely to be positive, and they will carry away the feeling that they have just visited a successful school.

Any experienced teacher or administrator knows that there's a distinct difference in the feel/smell/look of a good and thriving school compared to a mediocre one. People often describe what they perceive to be a "good" school as one that has a "friendly climate—a climate of success," and conversely describe the mediocre one as being simply "bad," a school "that just doesn't feel right." Consider this: A study comparing highly successful and less successful corporations noted that high-performing companies have a *culture* of pride and a *climate* of success. The study defined culture of pride as an emotional and value commitment between person and organization; people feel they belong to a meaningful entity and can realize cherished values by their contributions. Organizations that capture a culture of pride tend to be successful because their cultures foster a climate of success (Kanter, 1983, p. 149).

Although we measure the climate in a school or district by examining its culture, ecology, cast of characters, and social system, without your personal cultivation—without your leadership—the positive climate tapestry you want to weave won't evolve on its own. It's your responsibility to weave and promote an image of your school that demonstrates and supports effective teaching and learning, promotes positive employee and student attitudes and motivation, and elicits visitor and patron descriptors such as "great place," "welcoming environment," and so on. Although the district worries about its overall image in the climate paradigm, you can create your school's own positive climate with the tools you have available on site. Your leadership behavior is the starting point, and you must be energetic and lively as you move your school toward its goals. The leadership/management climate of success you create should be inviting to all who work in, as well as visit, your building.

Gaining Autonomy in the Bureaucracy

Your state prescribes the areas in which your school district's board of education and superintendent have autonomy. This is a form of *directed* autonomy and gives your district the freedom to set and enforce policy in specific areas. Examples include:

Districtwide policies	State relations	Contract enforcement
General budget	Legal services	Transportation services
Capital improvement	Food services	Facility management
Personnel administration		

School districts usually share with building-level administrators (principals) some of the following without granting full directed autonomy:

Vision and planning	Resource distribution	Curriculum adoption
Coordination of services	Community relations	Building maintenance
Employment of faculty and staff		

And just as the school district has directed autonomy, principals function, for the most part, within limits prescribed for them. Such prescriptions originate from various sources, that is, board of education mandates; superintendents' discretion; and district rules, regulations, policies, and procedures. These same limits are validated through adherence by peers and followers. For example:

Curriculum and instruction	Performance evaluation	Codes of conduct
Instructional priorities	Activity funds	Teacher roles
Performance expectations	Record keeping	Annual calendar
	Policy enforcement	Budget management
		Faculty maintenance

And just as districts share some directed autonomy with principals, principals, in turn, share some of their directed autonomy with faculty and staff. Some examples include:

Staff development	Curriculum design	Program evaluation
Student conduct	Community relations	Vision and planning
Daily schedule	Budget development	

Finally, faculty and staff have some of their own directed autonomy. For example:

Instructional methods	Learning goals
Use of technology	Supplemental instructional materials
Student assessment	Instructional priorities (rapidly being
Grading practices	replaced by "test teaching")

It's interesting to note that although your authority to do your job is clear—with your fixed limits, or directed autonomy, as principal having been set by your superiors—the methods for operating within your prescribed limits can be quite ambiguous. And although ambiguity can be scary for anyone who aspires to be a manager, it's the first thing a potential leader notes. "Aha! Directed autonomy without clearly defined methods of action!" This ambiguity is one of the early signals that a principal can be more than just a manager and, in fact, become exemplary as a leader. It's the loophole that allows you to "be yourself" and to make many of your own decisions. It's an opportunity to expand your sphere of autonomy. Here's why.

First, ambiguity in mandated policy or procedures can lead to some personal, on-the-job autonomy. Second, although you certainly have limits on your professional behavior, nobody has really set any limits on your personal behavior. Third, not all situations can be handled by routine, ritualized behavior. And fourth, manager/ principals manage and maintain the status quo, whereas leader/ principals innovate, within group limits, and try to meet the needs of individuals. What does this mean?

We know that in almost any group, the limits of behavior tolerated for one individual may be quite different from those tolerated for another or even for the group as a whole. Let's examine two hypothetical principals for a moment.

Principal Jones is decisive; keeps superiors, peers, and followers informed; has a high success rating on specific tasks; is sensitive to the needs of followers and constituents; and often demonstrates *idiosyncratic* (unique, autonomous) behavior in the operation of the school.

In comparison, Principal Smith, although he also has a high success rating on specific tasks, is slow to react; often calls superiors for advice; can be dictatorial; and seldom varies from rules, regulations, policies, or procedures in the operation of the school. "Old by-the-book Smith," we call him!

Now, both principals have a high success rating on specific tasks, but one principal, Principal Jones, involves followers in decisions, demonstrates sensitivity, and looks for creative solutions— albeit idiosyncratic at times—to task-related problems. He seldom seeks advice from superiors. He is, according to social scientists and researchers, accumulating "group-awarded idiosyncrasy credit" that can then be "spent" in support of additional "idiosyncratic" behavior before group sanctions are applied (Hollander, 1958). In other words, effective principals function within the limits of their group-accorded idiosyncrasy credit. If the situation to be resolved is one in which (a) personal ingenuity plays a significant role, (b) the resolution of the problem falls within the limits imposed by superiors, and (c) the problem is solved, then the principal will be able to make a deposit to his or her banked idiosyncrasy credit. But—and this is extremely important to remember—any situation that shows incompetence will result in a *withdrawal* of credit. When the balance is exhausted, group sanctions by superiors and followers will be quickly imposed. That's a euphemism for the word "canned."

An abundance of credits, combined with a record of success, allows effective principals to move through their day-to-day operations with a certain amount of gained autonomy from the ever-watchful eyes of superiors and followers. And that's what effective principals strive for—a certain amount of personal authority, a certain amount of autonomy. "After all," Principal Jones might say,

> you hired me to do a job. Now, let me do it, my way, within policy limits. If you're going to hold me accountable, let me have the freedom to develop programs and interpret policy in a manner that fits the needs of my followers and community. And, by the way—what's with this mandated zero-tolerance stuff that doesn't credit me with the intelligence to make reasonable decisions?

There is a considerable degree of personal discretion built into any school district's administrative structure. You have to find it and then, by careful application, earn such freedom. Perhaps the charts in Figure 4.1 will make the importance of autonomy stand out in your mind. But again, be cautious!

THE BOTTOM LINE

Multiple constituencies, a tangled web of interrelationships, antagonistic forces, perilous equilibrium, primary allegiance, identifying a skillful mentor, formal and informal authority structures, perpetual chaos, climate, bureaucracy, autonomy—Yipes! My head

Figure 4.1.

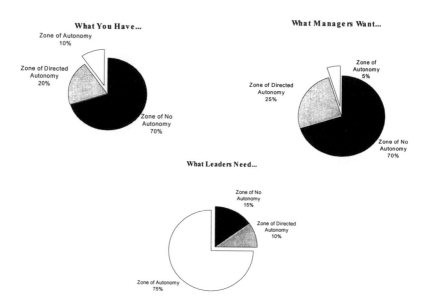

What You Have...

Zone of Autonomy
10%

Zone of Directed
Autonomy
20%

Zone of No
Autonomy
70%

What Managers Want...

Zone of
Autonomy
5%

Zone of Directed
Autonomy
25%

Zone of No
Autonomy
70%

What Leaders Need...

Zone of No
Autonomy
15%

Zone of Directed
Autonomy
10%

Zone of Autonomy
75%

is spinning. What am I getting into? I just want to work with kids, and teachers, and parents, and—well, why do I need to know how to deal with all of this?

The answer is simple. Without some grasp of the meaning of your relationship to the whole, it's not going to be easy for you to gain and keep

- A vivid sense of your own capacity to act as an individual
- A sure sense of your own dignity
- An awareness of your role(s) and responsibilities

Without an understanding of the culture you work in and the ability to experience success in that culture, you're liable to become a *spectator* and sink into passivity rather than becoming an competent *actor*—an effective principal (paraphrased from Gardner, 1963, p. 59). That's the first bottom line! Here's the second, again, coequal.

You're considering a position that, by all definitions, contains some of the toughest tasks anyone can imagine, and you will be besieged with problems that need a judicious principal to resolve. The synonyms for judicious include prudent, politic, practical, sensible, discrete, and expedient. Think of just such synonyms as you read the following, and before you turn to the next chapters.

The Toughest Job in the World

It can be more fatiguing than a day of stonecutting . . .
It can be more nerve wracking than a day of heart surgery . . .
It can bring success, happiness, death . . .
In today's security-conscious society, fewer people want to
    tackle it . . .
It's not a job for those who are afraid to fail . . .
It's not a job for the reckless, who can be dangerous . . .
It invites ridicule, criticism, and unpopularity . . .
But without it the world stands still . . .
It is the lonely, precarious job of making decisions.[1]

NOTE

1. Author and date unknown.

REFERENCES

Belasco, J. A. (1990). *Teaching the elephant to dance: Empowering change in your organization.* New York: Crown.

Blumberg, A., & Greenfield, W. (1980). *The effective principal: Perspectives on school leadership.* Boston: Allyn & Bacon.

Carroll, L. (1992). *Alice's adventures in wonderland and through the looking glass.* New York: Dell.

Clemmer, E. F. (1991). *The school policy handbook.* Boston: Allyn & Bacon.

Donaldson, G. A. (1991). *Learning to lead: The dynamics of the high school principalship.* Westport, CT: Greenwood.

Erlandson, D. A. (1994). *Building a career: Fulfilling the lifetime professional needs of principals.* Fairfax, VA: National Policy Board for Educational Administration.

Gardner, J. W. (1963). *Self-renewal: The individual and the innovative society.* New York: Harper & Row.

Gleick, J. (1988). *Chaos: Making a new science.* New York: Viking Penguin.

Hall, G. E., & Parkay, F. W. (1992). Reflections on becoming a principal. In F. W. Parkay & G. E. Hall (Eds.), *Becoming a principal: The challenges of beginning leadership.* Boston: Allyn & Bacon.

Hollander, E. P. (1958). Conformity, status, and idiosyncrasy credit. *Psychological Review, 65*(2), 117-127.

Imber, M., & Van Geel, T. (1993). *Education law.* New York: McGraw-Hill.

Kanter, R. M. (1983). *The change masters: Innovation and entrepreneurship in the American Corporation.* New York: Simon & Schuster.

Kowalski, T. (1999). *The school superintendent: Theory, practice and cases.* Englewood Cliffs, NJ: Prentice Hall.

Miskel, C., & Ogawa, R. (1988). Work motivation, job satisfaction, and climate. In N. Boyan (Ed.), *Handbook of research on educational administration* (pp. 279-304). New York: Longman.

Morris, R. L., Crowson, R., Porter-Gehrie, C., & Hurwitz, E. (1984). *Principals in action.* Columbus, OH: Merrill.

Owens, R. G. (1998). *Organizational behavior in education* (6th ed.). Boston: Allyn & Bacon.

Rutherford, W. L. (1985). School principals as effective leaders. *Phi Delta Kappan, 67*(1), 31-34.

Taguiri, R. (1968). The concept of organizational climate. In R. Taguiri & G. Litwin (Eds.), *Organizational climate: Explorations of a concept* (pp. 11-32). Boston: Harvard University, Graduate School of Business, Division of Research.

Vaill P. (1989). *Managing as a performing art.* San Francisco: Jossey-Bass.

Waller, W. (1965). *The sociology of teaching.* New York: John Wiley.

Walsh, P. (1998, December 6). A effort, but F for far too much of it. *Washington Post,* p. C5.

Weber, M. (1964). *The theory of social and economic organizations* (T. Parsons, Ed., A. M. Henderson & T. Parsons, Trans.). New York: Free Press. (Original work published 1910)

Wiles, D., Wiles, J., & Bondi, J. (1980). *Practical politics for school administrators.* Boston: Allyn & Bacon.

5

Are You Listening?

Do You Understand?

ABOUT THIS CHAPTER

Kathleen Hirsch (1998) writes,

> We move in a river of talk. We *are* the stories we tell one another, the myths we live by. So much of who we are comes from the stew of plots over which those before us have argued fiercely, shaded and shaped and simply come to claim. Because our days in a place deposit their own truths like minerals in our bones. (p. 8)

Clearly, she's right. You *are* moving in a river of talk. You're in a profession where talk is your main tool. But there are a whole lot of people who are counting on you to listen to what they say and to interpret their messages in a way that assures them that you understand and care. To do so, you must listen carefully and thoughtfully to their concerns and interests. Effective principals use careful listening to gain direct access to their followers' most pressing concerns (Marlow, 1992).

AUTHOR'S NOTE: Much of the research for this chapter was done by Jeannine Tate, an administrator in the Fairfax County, Virginia, public schools and a doctoral candidate at George Mason University.

REFLECTIVE POINT

*Before they can draw conclusions concerning your sense
of purpose or ability to get things done, potential followers
must have a sense of trust in you. One of the best ways
to build trust is by careful listening.*

In your quest to become or remain an effective principal, you need to understand the day-to-day experiences and concerns of your faculty and staff. You need to carefully listen to what members of your organization worry about, are motivated by, and are frustrated by and you need to sense what they feel and want as they go about their work.

There are a number of characteristics that potential followers look for in effective principals. The paramount ones nearly always hinge on followers' perceptions that you demonstrate a strong sense of purpose and the ability to get things done. But before they can draw conclusions about your sense of purpose or ability to lead, potential followers must develop trust in you. One of the best ways to build trust is by listening. When people feel they are being heard, you tap into one of the most powerful dynamics of human interaction.

THE ART AND SKILLS OF
CAREFUL LISTENING

Lee Iacocca stated, "I only wish I could find an institute that teaches people how to listen. After all, a good manager needs to listen at least as much as he [sic] needs to talk. Too many people fail to realize that good communication goes in both directions" (cited in Purdy, 1997, p. 2).

There's a high cost for poor communication in organizations, and the main culprit in perpetuating poor communication frequently is the standard operating procedure of calling a meeting to disburse information and make decisions. Often—no, not just often, *usually*, certain members monopolize meetings, and the same old business is rehashed endlessly (Ellinor & Gerard, 1998). To make matters worse, members interpret what transpires according to their own experiences, expectations, and perspectives. Therefore, little is done to advance collaborative thinking, much less mutual understanding, among members of the organization, and the opportunity for partnership and the advancement of organizational goals is lost.

If effective leading is about bringing people together to accomplish specific goals and recognizing and appreciating different perspectives, then leading requires collaboration in which all members of the organization are open to listening to others and being influenced by them—listening to reflect and learn before decisions are made.

Many social scientists have agreed that we don't need more or different theories in management studies, but rather a better understanding of conversations and conversational realities. Effective principals are not successful because they find and apply brilliant theories. They are successful because they are able to sort out and make intelligent sense of the disordered jumble of impressions they must deal with daily. This ability to construct sensible meaning begins with *deep listening* (Shotter, 1993).

"Deep," or careful, listening is more complex than the physiological act of hearing—it is a dynamic mental act. A careful listener is one who sincerely wants to listen and demonstrates both patience while listening and a willingness to be of assistance to the speaker. To be a careful listener, you must listen respectfully and attend to the emotions, needs, and concerns of the person speaking (Purdy, 1997). You must learn to interpret cues and make sense of the speaker's message in terms of your own experiences. Careful listeners adapt to the varied communication styles of speakers and recognize that meanings change from person to person and situation to situation.

The following is probably more than you ever wanted to know about the subject of careful listening, but it substantiates the importance of learning to listen in a number of different ways. Psychologists and communication experts have identified numerous styles of listening. The simplest is *discriminative listening,* in which one listens in order to distinguish aural stimulation (emotional nature of the speaker's tone). *Comprehensive listening* is when one listens for an understanding of the message. *Critical evaluative listening* takes place when one wants to make an intelligent response to a persuasive message. *Therapeutic listening* is a nonjudgmental way of listening with the interests of the speaker in mind. The effective principal doesn't treat these listening styles as separate entities, but rather filters messages incorporating all four styles as one.

There are many other styles and theories of listening, and while the authorities who espouse them might disagree, they all seem to fit into the paradigm described above. Often the most relaxing is *appreciative listening,* in which the message is enjoyed for its own sake (Purdy, 1997). Others, among many more, include *active listening* (Farson, 1996), *analytical listening* (Helgesen, 1990), *empathetic listening* (Brownell, 1993; Bruneau, 1993), *tangible, visceral way of being informed* (Peters & Austin, 1985), deep listening (Helgesen, 1990), *intrapersonal and extrapersonal listening and communication-decentering* (Johnson, 1993), *logico-experimental function* (Roethlesbieger, 1995), and *gender differences* (Borisoff & Hahn, 1997; Helgesen, 1995). This is clearly an impressive list of theories; the bottom line, however, is simply this: Effective principals exhibit strong, careful listening behaviors in their day-to-day activities.

Listening in a Nonlinear Culture

Now, we know that the principal's job is seldom linear. Look at the two statements that follow and think about how difficult, but critical, it is to cultivate careful listening skills.

> *Statement 1:* Most administrative activities are short, fragmented, and verbal (Bogotch & Roy, 1997), and principals find themselves constantly involved in events that are initiated by *interruptions* (I call them "hiccups").

"Well, I already know that," you say, *"So that's what we mean by 'nonlinear'! So then, how does Statement 1 relate to careful listening?"* It's simple, but very important. An interruption causes a predictable sequence of events. Let's say you're in the middle of listening to Betty, and suddenly you're interrupted by Ted.

> **Betty:** "Richard [that's you], I think that we should be looking at making some major changes in our curriculum to meet the required skills necessary for our kids to pass the state Standards of Learning. First, I suggest that we closely exam-

ine both our vertical articulation as well as our horizontal articulation before we embark on . . ."

Ted: "Richard, Betty, I'm sorry to interrupt but—well, there's a leak in the ceiling in my room!"

Now, you've got two people to accommodate at the same time and you don't want to short-change either of them. You've been interrupted while you've been carefully listening to Betty. You were in the act of trying to fully comprehend and build the factual foundation you need to resolve her concern. You now have Betty's unfinished narrative in your mind while you're receiving entirely different information and concerns from Ted.

Ted: "And it's dripping on the new carpet!"

You lay Betty's case aside to hear what Ted has to say. Now, you quickly move into a phase of "progressive retrieval" (Gronn, 1983). In other words, Ted has exhausted his vocalization of the problem, and you've put Ted's needs foremost in your mind—at the expense of Betty—and now you're ready to make an informed and immediate decision to resolve Ted's concerns.

You: "There's a bucket in the custodian closet, Ted. You go get it while I send a custodian to your room."

Clearly, Ted's dilemma requires "careful listening," but not much more than a "bucket approach." A substantial number of school-based "hiccups" do require more than just a bucket, however—they require considerate, careful listening to produce a positive outcome. You need to contact a custodian as promised, but then you must regenerate your conversation with Betty.

You: "Sorry 'bout that, Betty. Where were we?"

Betty will probably start her conversation from the beginning, and you will be able to restart your listening process from the beginning. If she doesn't, and if you've lost what she previously said, it's important to prompt her to start over. You need all the information you can get so that you can provide the best possible response.

Figure 5.1.

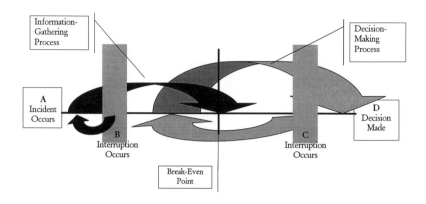

Keeping Statement 1 in mind, look at Statement 2:

Statement 2: Principals make the poorest decisions when they are interrupted early in the listening process or late in the decision-making process. (Figure 5.1 illustrates the problem with interruption and fragmented listening/ decision-making processes. It also illustrates how the "art" of careful listening works.)

Confused? Let's dissect Figure 5.1 using the Betty, Ted, and "You" scenario as a foundation.

Point A. An incident occurs. Betty proceeds to give you, the decision maker, information that you need to help resolve the matter. In a perfect world, Betty would be able to proceed to the Break-Even Point without interruption. You, then, would start at the same Break-Even Point and be able to think through the decision-making process and arrive at Point D (Decision Made) also without interruption. This is not very likely in the real world of school administration. Effective principals, that is, careful listeners, know how to deal with, and around, distraction.

Point B. Ted interrupts. You deal with the interruption and then return to Betty. If you believe that Betty had presented almost all of her concerns to you before the interruption, and if you believe that you were able to retain those concerns, then you and Betty can pick up from where you left off. If not, you and Betty must restart the speaking/listening process from Point A.

Note. The most important points that Betty wanted you to hear were probably stated during the upward thrust of the Information-Gathering Process arrow in Figure 5.1. If you're interrupted at Point B, you probably should restart the conversation from Point A. You can assume, however, that points made during the downward thrust of the Information-Gathering Process arrow were reiterations. You may be able to continue directly to the Break-Even Point without loss of information. Notice that your Decision-Making Process can start during Betty's reiteration process. There's an overlap between the end of the Information-Gathering Process arrow and the start of the Decision-Making Process arrow in Figure 5.1. Be cautious, however, and don't rush this overlap. You must still be giving Betty your full attention without any signs of interruption until she reaches the Break-Even Point.

Point C. If you, the decision maker, are interrupted at this point, you may have to start your part of the process over to recall bits and pieces of your line of thinking. If, however, you're on the downward thrust of the Decision-Making Process arrow when you're interrupted, you can assume that you're in your own reiteration process and continue without much backtracking.

Point D. You've been a careful listener. In your mind, you've measured all the salient points; you've weighed potential outcomes, considering all of your infamous multiple constituencies; and you've pictured your potential decision within the overall culture you're working with, and in. Now comes your decision.

You: "Betty, let's do it! I like your suggestions. Let me know what you need from me. Betty, is that—is that water I see trickling around the corner?"

The Often-Forgotten Part of Careful Listening

Returning to Figure 5.1 for a moment, recall that during the Information-Gathering Process speakers normally provide the most important *physical* information for the decision maker during the upward thrust of the arrow and mostly reiterate during the downward thrust. Equally important, but often overlooked or dismissed, is the speaker's *collateral* or *resultant emotional level*. Often, after the immediate physical facts have been presented, the arrow's upward thrust continues to climb, fueled by the speaker's emotional involvement. If you, as a decision maker, become overly attuned to gathering just the facts of an incident, you may overlook the emotional baggage the speaker is carrying into the description of the incident or problem. For example, let's add the following declaratory statements to Ted's dilemma. First, Ted told you in very few words, "There's a leak in the ceiling in my room—and it's dripping on the new carpet!" You heard: "leak," "ceiling," Ted's "room," and perhaps "new carpet." That's about all you needed to hear in this situation to make your decision. Now, consider if Ted had added such statements as, "My whole day is ruined!" "It's a conspiracy!" "I think someone is out to ruin my reputation as a teacher!" Or "Some of the water, or whatever it is, splashed on me and now I'm feeling feverish!" Ridiculous, you say? Not so. You're dealing with human emotions or perceptions, not just cold, hard physical facts. What you don't know is what might have happened in Ted's life prior to the immediate incident—problems at home that morning with spouse, car, and so on or problems that Ted had after arriving at school that morning, for example, with another faculty or staff member or with students. While you're collecting physical facts about the incident, it's imperative that you also sense the speaker's tone of voice, body language, and other clues or cues presented to you spontaneously coupled with the speaker's presentation of facts.

Effective, careful listening is concerned with not just the physical problem at hand but also the emotional dilemma it may be causing the speaker. In Ted's case, a bucket and a custodian will satisfy the physical situation. But if you add emotional state into the paradigm, you would have to tell Betty that you'll continue your conversation with her later. Attending to Ted's emotional stability is the new and immediate priority.

If you really want to understand what the speaker is trying to communicate, you must assume that the speaker is expressing his or her true feelings and sentiments. Words alone are not the actual sentiments even though the speaker is using words to express them. You must assume that you can't understand another's feelings and sentiments until you find the context for them. You must look for a referent to the speaker's words in life events and social situations to understand the real meaning of those words.

Blocks to Effective Listening

For years, communication experts have studied blocks to careful listening. Inhibitors to careful listening include leading questions, unsolicited advice, defensiveness, clichés, and premature judgment. Listeners contribute to a defensive climate when they evaluate the speaker or the speaker's ideas. If listeners attempt to control the conversation or exhibit an attitude of superiority or dogmatism, listening is blocked. On the other hand, an air of neutrality or uninvolvement is not conducive to listening either. A supportive listening climate is one in which the listener is nonjudgmental. Judgment, defined here, is that which is stored in our memory banks. When pieces of data trigger a memory, they are acted on without conscious thought. Judgment makes it difficult for listeners to stay open to alternative views. Listeners' egos become identified with how they think things are, and they tend to defend their own positions. In doing so, they close themselves off from other positions, and they just state their own opinions more loudly (Ellinor & Gerard, 1998). In other words, a careful listener's behavior is spontaneous and noncalculating. Careful listeners empathize with the speaker and create an air of equality, mutual respect, and trust.

Listening as a Responsive Process

It's been said that careful listening is the single most powerful creative act one can perform. This is a bit of an overstatement, but individuals do listen and create reality based on what they hear. It is the doorway through which we allow the world to enter. We frame our perspective of reality in how we listen, to what and to whom we listen, and the assumptions through which we listen (Bennis, 1997). Listening is not a passive process. In a conversation, at least two people take turns speaking and listening. For example, you pass teacher Jones in the hall between class:

> **Teacher Jones** proclaims: "I am really hot today!" (You quickly process such things as hot flashes, mosquito bites at their worst, anger, room temperature, acute jock itch, hair, makeup, clothing—*you need more information* before you make a response.)

> **You:** "Really?" (Now you're probing for *more info, please!* Or you could just jump into the conversation by making an *uninformed* remark such as, "Have you thought about seeing a doctor? Or, "Perhaps some ointment might bring you some relief?")

> **Teacher Jones:** "Yes," she replies with a big smile, "The new lesson plan I've unveiled in my first two classes today is really working well! I'm so pleased!" Aha! Finally, you have the information you need to respond appropriately. Now you can respond with a nod of approval while you safely and sincerely state:

> **You:** "I'm pleased, too."

You need to recognize that every word in a conversation is a response to another word in an active process. When listeners perceive and understand the meaning of speech, they assume a responsive attitude toward it. Listeners either agree or disagree with the statement made by the speaker. Then the listeners personalize the statement, apply it, and prepare a response (Shotter, 1993).

At the same time, the speaker actively expects some kind of response, such as agreement, sympathy, a challenge, criticism, or the like. Each speaker continuously reacts to the response of the other. To understand one another, conversation is a negotiated, back-and-forth process.

You must understand that every face-to-face interaction contains and produces concepts of partial truths. Not everything can be presented at all times, and we make ongoing judgments about what we hear. Conversations are reciprocal chain-linked processes in which we receive partial meanings from what others say and give part of that meaning back (Bogotch & Roy, 1997).

Listening for Shared Meaning

As an effective principal, you must listen carefully for shared meaning between the participants of any conversation. The primary function of speech is to give shape, to maintain, reproduce, or transform certain modes of personal and social relationships—to position people in relation to each other. Meanings depend on the situation and the people in the situation. Shared meaning is not easy to negotiate. Because what is being talked about comes from at least two sets of experiences, the participants must offer each other the opportunity to contribute to the making of the shared meaning (Shotter, 1993).

Listening for collective shared meaning assumes that what each individual feels, sees, hears, and perceives is a window on a common reality. Listening can improve individual relationships, and careful listening can improve relationships in any organization. Listening carefully for shared meaning doesn't just happen, it's a *skill and an art*. You need to learn to listen without preconceived notions of what you will hear. You need to learn to look at situations from different perspectives. When you listen for the interrelationships among all the perceptions, the whole becomes visible. By listening to a group to find collective meaning, you expand your understanding and develop new possibilities for the organization.

As an effective principal, you can examine collective shared meanings to learn the norms and assumptions that guide the group's decisions and actions. You can listen for how members are rewarded and the priorities that repeatedly get the group's attention and gather clues about organizational culture by watching to see whose presence is necessary for the group to function well and how decisions are made.

It's your role to act as a boundary spanner among the multiple constituencies in your school and school district. Many problems in organizations have their bases in misunderstanding. Generally, people assume that everyone has had the same experiences and that words have the same meaning for everyone. This is seldom true. You must recognize differences as well as similarities among your constituencies. You need to learn to ask appropriate questions while listening carefully, so that each individual's unique view is taken into account.

THE BOTTOM LINE

If you want to listen so you really hear what others say, make sure you're not a

- *Mind reader.* You'll hear little or nothing as you think, "What is this person really thinking or feeling?"
- *Rehearser.* Your mental tryouts for "Here's what I'll say next" tune out the speaker.
- *Filterer.* Some call this selective listening—hearing only what you want to hear.
- *Dreamer.* Drifting off during a face-to-face conversation can lead to an embarrassing, "What did you say?" or "Could you repeat that?"
- *Identifier.* If you refer everything you hear to your experience, you probably didn't really hear what was said.
- *Comparer.* When you get sidetracked assessing the messenger, you're sure to miss the message.
- *Derailer.* Changing the subject too quickly tells others you're not interested in anything they have to say.
- *Sparrer.* You hear what's said but quickly belittle it or discount it. That puts you in the same class as the derailer.
- *Placater.* Agreeing with everything you hear just to be nice or to avoid conflict does not mean you're a good listener. (Writing Lab, n.d.)

So—hello. Are you listening?

REFERENCES

Bennis, W. (1997). *Managing people is like herding cats.* Provo, UT: Executive Excellence Publishing.

Bogotch, I. E., & Roy, C. P. (1997). The contexts of partial truths: An analysis of principals' discourse. *Journal of Educational Administration, 35,* 234-252.

Borisoff, D., & Hahn, D. F. (1997). Listening and gender: Values revalued. In D. Borisoff & D. H. Hahn (Eds.), *Listening in everyday life: A personal and professional approach* (pp. 55-75). Lanham, MD: University Press of America.

Brownell, J. (1993). Listening environment: A perspective. In A. D. Wolvin & C. G. Coakley (Eds.), *Perspectives on listening* (pp. 241-260). Norwood, NJ: Ablex.

Bruneau, T. (1993). Empathy and listening. In A. D. Wolvin & C. G. Coakley (Eds.), *Perspectives on listening* (pp. 185-200). Norwood, NJ: Ablex.

Ellinor, L., & Gerard, G. (1998). *Dialogue: Rediscover the transforming power of conversation.* New York: John Wiley.

Farson, R. (1996). *Management of the absurd.* New York: Touchstone.

Gronn, P. (1983). Talk as work: The accomplishments of school administration. *Administrative Science Quarterly, 28,* 1-21.

Helgesen, S. (1990). *The female advantage: Women's ways of leadership.* New York: Doubleday Currency.

Helgesen, S. (1995). *The web of inclusion.* New York: Doubleday Currency.

Hirsch, K. (1998). *A home in the heart of a city.* New York: Farrar, Straus & Giroux

Johnson, J. (1993). Functions and process of inner speech in listening. In A. D. Wolvin & C. G. Coakley (Eds.), *Perspectives on listening* (pp. 29-53). Norwood, NJ: Ablex.

Marlow, M. (1992). Inspiring trust. *Executive Excellence, 9*(12), 12-15.

Peters, T., & Austin, N. (1985). *A passion for excellence: The leadership difference.* New York: Random House.

Purdy, M. (1997). What is listening? In M. Purdy & D. Borisoff (Eds.), *Listening in everyday life: A personal and professional approach* (pp. 1-16). Lanham, MD: University Press of America.

Roethlesbieger, F. J. (1995). Of words and men. In S. T. Corman, S. P. Banks, C. R. Bantz, & M. E. Meyer (Eds.), *Foundations of organizational communication* (pp. 88-96). White Plains, NY: Longman.

Shotter, J. (1993). *Conversational realities: Construction life through language.* Thousand Oaks, CA: Sage.

Writing Lab. (n.d.). Purdue University, Department of English.

6

Let's Talk
Aggregate Impression

How Leaders Lead

ABOUT THIS CHAPTER

If you're not cautious, the continuing trend toward professionalism in management as the panacea for getting things done can and will handicap you in the development of your leadership skills. Most of the current and popular leadership theories, assessment methods, and state certification mandates are based on management tasks. Now, any observer who makes this kind of a broad-brush declaration knows full well that this is an invitation to an often "bloodletting" debate. Chances are good, however, that during your formal education leadership coursework, leadership was not always framed as a delicate art. Rather, leadership may have been discussed as a science—the science of *management* in administration. In addition, mentors will talk about leadership in terms of "accepted prac-

---

AUTHOR'S NOTE: This chapter is adapted from Dunklee, D. R. (1998). How Leaders Lead: A New Look at Leadership Behavior With Implications for Identification and Development. *The AASA Professor: Research and Best Practices That Advance the Profession of Educational Administration*, 21(3/4), 4-14.

tice." If you critically examine current practice, you'll find abundant examples of this focus on management. For example, you may be persuaded to think

- Leadership is defined as your competence in implementing and enforcing standard operating procedures (SOPs) and your leadership skills will be measured by how well you keep the lid on the place, raise test scores, and follow SOPs. Note: This concept of leadership is pure management and yet is frequently presented as "administrative leadership" or "instructional leadership."

- Your success as an education leader is predicated on your successful adaptation to existing organizational forces and priorities. Note: In other words, your preparation as a potential leader is, for the most part, an apprenticeship in folklore and current practice—"It's always been that way"; "This is the way we do it."

But schools, school districts, and other organizations really need more than managers, more than folklore-based experts. They need true leaders who instead of merely perpetuating existing practice or historical traditions, envision productive new ways of achieving organizational goals and instituting requisite changes. You can rise above existing practice and historical traditions if you understand that although it's important for you to have a working knowledge of the history and traditions of the organization, focusing solely on this knowledge tends to promote a "steady management" paradigm and can stifle your efforts to become an effective leader. As a leader in the education ranks, you'll be more difficult to identify than you think. To be an effective principal/leader, you will have to first prove yourself as an effective principal/manager. You'll have a difficult time being recognized as a leader, however, because you're going to be extremely busy doing what you've have been trained for and are expected to do: manage. Remember the example of the line cook in Chapter 1? You must flip the burgers before you can be acknowledged as a full-fledged chef. You must be able to keep the lid on the place, raise test scores, and of course follow SOPs.

Many preparation institutions still reinforce the emphasis on training managers and perpetuate a "compliance" mentality as the model for leadership—ignoring visionary thinking, calculated risk taking, and other key leadership prerogatives and identifiers. You may need to master management skills separately, as a corollary to leadership.

Okay, enough exhortation. Simply stated, this chapter is limited to the discussion of *leadership*. The next chapter will present a parallel discussion of *management*.

The learning objectives outlined at the beginning of the previous chapters, along with the follow-up discussions of the various "cultures," were all prerequisites to this chapter. This chapter pulls those learning objectives together and examines the art of leadership through a leader profile that illustrates leadership behavior in both normative and summative form while carefully omitting management or administration descriptors. It presents an opportunity for you to take a fresh look at the capabilities and behaviors that define effective leaders. The chapter introduces you to *aggregate impression* leadership—a practitioner-based model that suggests how you can achieve and maintain status as a leader over time.

REFLECTIVE POINT

Leadership as defined in this chapter is based on five interrelated assumptions:

1. There are identifiable competencies and behaviors that will distinguish you as a leader, not just a manager/administrator.
2. Regardless of the knowledge and skills, competencies and behaviors you exhibit, leadership is possible only when other people (i.e., followers) grant you the power to lead.
3. People will grant leader status to you based on their perceptions of who you are, what you stand for (shared values and beliefs), and the degree to which you can be trusted to speak and act effectively on their behalf.
4. Others' perceptions of you develop over time as people observe and interpret your behaviors and actions in a variety of situations and circumstances.

5. Applying the tenets of this chapter to your behavior and remaining continuously aware of the perception development process of others, you can consciously reinforce the aggregate impression of your leader status in the eyes of potential followers.

LEADERSHIP: WHAT IS IT?
WHY DO WE NEED LEADERS?
WHAT DO LEADERS DO?
HOW DO LEADERS DO WHAT THEY DO?

Why Another New Look at Leadership Theory?

As mentioned previously, most of the current popular leadership theories are primarily management theories that provide no clear way to identify what sets leaders apart. Yet, there is not only a difference between management and leadership (including the generic term administration), they are mutually exclusive. One *manages* tasks, activities, and the human and material resources to maintain business as usual. One *leads* people to improve or enhance business or to develop and implement change. A manager is an "individual who utilizes existing structures or procedures to achieve an organizational goal or objective." The manager "is concerned primarily with maintaining, rather than changing established structures, procedures, or goals." In contrast, the leader "is concerned with initiating changes in established structures, procedures, or goals; he [sic] is a disrupter of the existing state of affairs" (Lipham, 1964, p. 122).

The more leadership research you read, the clearer the difference between leading and managing becomes. Whereas managers often involve people in various ways in making decisions, leaders go beyond that: Leaders create and communicate a vision that inspires followers (see Bennis & Namus, 1998; Burns, 1985; Owens, 1998; Schmidt & Finnegan, 1992). The goal of leadership is to build human buy-in to an idea, a vision, an objective in such a way that the participants are inspired and motivated by unity of purpose and mutually shared values. Although in a best case scenario effective leaders are also effective managers, there are situations where history designates as effective leaders people who have extremely poor managerial skills. In such cases, research demonstrates that these leaders surrounded themselves with highly effective managers and delegated most, if not all, managerial tasks. You will be most effective as a school administrator if you can both manage *and* lead. And if you surround yourself with talented subordinates—you have the best of all worlds.

If you were to examine the multitude of leadership theories that have been promulgated during the past decade, you would see an intermixture of management tasks and leadership skills. For example, leadership is often defined by statements such as: "motivate others to . . ., " "arouse others' personal commitment to . . .," "organize the environment to . . .," "facilitate the work that . . . ." Here is a perfect example of the amalgamation of management and leadership. The first two statements describe what leaders do, the last statements describe what managers do. The difference is clear. Leaders seek to influence or change the behavior of other people; managers work with existing behaviors and organize and maintain routine work efforts. Leaders influence; managers implement and administer. Leaders motivate; managers facilitate.

Contrary to some prevalent views concerning management versus leadership, it's clear that one can lead without disrupting, that change and growth can be subtle rather than drastic, and that the expectations of the organization can be integrated with the personal needs of those who support or work in the organization (Getzels, Lipham, & Campbell, 1968). So, the research that's presented to you in this chapter is a profile of absolute leadership (i.e., devoid of management descriptors), and how it evolves and is supported by followers. We'll examine absolute management in the next chapter.

Why Do We Need Leaders?

There are many instances in which people willingly empower others to make decisions and take action to bring about some desired outcome. Our need for leadership is a rational one. From early childhood on, we all face conflicts, and in spite of our preference for independence, we seek out individuals to make decisions or initiate action in areas where we lack competence or confidence. We tend to play the role of follower when it's obvious that someone else knows more about the problem to be resolved than we do. Leaders surface in times of confusion or lack of direction, or when we need someone to take responsibility, and they are more willing than we to accept responsibility. Leaders become visible when we abdicate; fail to act; or lack necessary skills, expertise, or understanding. Leaders function best when they possess or control the means to satisfy our needs as well as their own. Leaders function in social groups or systems through the use of influence, authority, or power (or a combination of all three). Our major focus in this chapter is the power of influence or perception over time, that is, aggregate impression.

How Do Leaders Lead?

Most researchers have concluded that leadership is generally granted to individuals who make a rational or emotional appeal to followers. This normative approach explains how a person is able to assume an immediate or short-term leadership role, but doesn't explain how that person maintains a leadership role over time. This book is concerned with long-term leadership and this chapter outlines a hypothesis that examines a summative approach to leadership. This summative approach is based on a normative platform, but focuses on the development of other people's perceptions and aggregate impressions. When leadership is predicated on, and limited to, the normative fundamentals of leadership, what we observe is really only a higher level of management. Long-term leadership is predicated on the leader's ability to identify, understand, respond to, and continuously manage the perceptions of others. To fully understand how leaders lead, you need to understand how people perceive.

Each of us has a perceptual screen though which we filter sensory stimuli and communications. Research shows that communication is not just words themselves, but also includes nonverbal factors such as touch, motion, posture, an artifact, time, color, or space (Rothlisberger, 1968). And further, as we work together with others, over time our perceptions and interpretations of each other tend to change or be modified. Recognizing this, leaders lead by understanding the effect our individual perceptual screens have on what we recognize as leadership (Sherif, 1967). They use this understanding to tailor the verbal and nonverbal messages they send and the roles they assume to reinforce our perception of their leader status. Although normative factors attend the process of leadership, summative perceptions and aggregate impression constitute its essence. No true leader can effectively maintain leadership by simply being an effective manager or following normative behaviors— or even by demonstrating qualities of charisma. Although these factors are certainly important, unless we perceive a person as a leader and unless the aggregate of our multiple diverse impressions over time creates a strong perception of leadership, the leader's power to lead steadily diminishes.

A powerful tool effective principals use to maintain their leadership status over time is to manage others' perceptions of their leadership by assuming different roles as changing circumstances dictate. We'll look at these two closely related concepts, aggregate impression and role assumption, in more detail later in this chapter.

A NEW LOOK AT LEADERSHIP[1]

As mentioned previously, this analysis of leadership theory (presented in hypothesis format in Note 2) is devoid of management skills and is limited to three very important, discernible competencies: *conceptual, anthropological,* and *technical.* Again, management skills will be examined separately in the next chapter. Below, I define these three leader competencies—conceptual, anthropological, and technical—in terms of the following requisite operative leader abilities. You'll want to carefully analyze your current competencies in relation to the ones identified below to see how close a match there is between who you are now and who you need to become for you to be recognized as an effective leader.

What Is Conceptual Competence?

Conceptual competence means having the operative[3] ability to

- See the enterprise as a whole, recognizing how the various functions of the organization depend on one another and how changes in any one part affect some or all of the others
- Understand the dynamics of leading and managing and the fact that leaders intentionally seek to influence the behavior of other people

- Perceive, value, know, act, and evaluate
- Understand that (a) leadership is voluntarily granted by followers who accept the leader's influence and direction, (b) leadership comes from the power that followers have willingly entrusted, and (c) followers are drawn to the ideas of the leader because they share in the values and beliefs of the leader and are convinced that the leader can represent the followers well
- Understand the difference between command or position power,[4] and leadership power[5]

What Is Anthropological Competence?

Anthropological competence means having the operative ability to

- Work effectively as a group member and build cooperative effort within the organization; understand that leadership is a group function that occurs only in the processes of two or more people interacting
- Advocate preferred outcomes and press for accomplishment
- Find pleasure in taking responsibility, holding power/authority; maintain a high capacity for work and work-related risk; employ superior coping mechanisms and a high tolerance for ambiguity
- Communicate, both orally and in writing, and practice superior interpersonal relations
- Balance emotional security, intellectual stimulation, and personal and professional satisfaction

What Is Technical Competence?

Technical competence means having the operative ability to

- Understand and be proficient in activities involving methods, processes, procedures, and techniques
- Build on both related and unrelated personal life experiences

- Maintain a strong, positive self-image that is not related to status
- Practice ongoing authenticity[6]
- Prioritize use of time for maximum effectiveness
- Maintain linear focus in nonlinear circumstances

Now that I've defined the three identified leader competencies—conceptual, anthropological, and technical—in terms of the requisite operative leader abilities, the next question is *how* do you act? What kind of behaviors do you need to exhibit to strengthen others' beliefs that you, indeed, have such competencies? Examples of leader behaviors[7] are described below under the headings of executive leadership, problem solving/decision making/judgment, sensitivity, and effective communication.

What Is Executive Leadership Behavior?

Executive leadership behavior occurs when a leader

- Demonstrates a sound understanding of the role of the enterprise in a democratic society; of philosophical and historical influences; of current cultural, social, political, economic, and global issues; and of other influences related to the enterprise
- Articulates a well-reasoned philosophy and system of values concerning the enterprise; promotes programs, policies, and procedures that are congruent with this philosophy and values system
- Demonstrates a sound understanding of the laws and regulations that affect the enterprise
- Demonstrates a sound understanding of the dynamics of local, state, and national politics, and the role of community leaders in the welfare of the enterprise
- Takes individual responsibility to promote a safe and secure working environment in the enterprise
- Leads the enterprise effectively by delineating responsibilities and authority, establishing multidirectional lines of communication

- Interprets the policies, directives, and actions of superiors (i.e., boards of education, leaders in higher positions); serves as a conduit between subordinates and superiors

- Sets priorities for the enterprise; develops goals with individuals and groups; provides leadership and guidance to remove obstacles and facilitate their accomplishment; initiates, plans, and actively leads organizational change; supports innovation

- Communicates a vision for the enterprise; builds commitment to plans of action; creates and channels energy toward common goals

- Recognizes and rewards effective performance; serves as a role model

- Identifies leadership for projects along with the authority and clearly defined goals necessary to accomplish them; follows up when necessary

- Is a visible leader; maintains frequent contact with subordinates at their work stations; consistently demonstrates support of subordinates and patrons

- Interacts effectively with groups; involves others in setting goals and solving problems; supports group decisions; knows when a group requires direction and applies effective facilitation skills

- Adapts leadership style to fit the varying needs of diverse personnel

- Is open to new ideas and change; conscientiously pursues opportunities for professional and personal growth and development; is knowledgeable about a variety of subjects (e.g., educational, political, current events, economic, cultural, etc.); actively participates in a variety of activities and events outside of the enterprise

- Performs well under pressure; demonstrates clear thinking and effective self-control in stressful situations; models linear behavior; monitors the physical and emotional climate; and reduces perceived crisis situations to normal operations and interactions

How Is Problem Solving/
Decision Making/Judgment Measured?

Leaders are effective when their behavior demonstrates the ability to

- Reach logical conclusions and make high-quality, timely decisions given the best possible information
- Consider the impact of decisions on other parts of the organization and correctly identify others who should be included in, or informed of, the problem-solving or decision-making process
- Accurately judge the importance and political impact of an issue or problem; set priorities and act accordingly; recognize the point at which a decision is required and act quickly
- Take reasonable, calculated risks to resolve problems in an effective and timely manner
- Recognize when problems cannot, or need not, be resolved and accept and adapt to the situation
- Maintain an open mind; consider differing points of view; assist others to form reasoned opinions about problems and issues

What Is Sensitivity?

Effective leaders demonstrate sensitivity when they

- Perceive and respond to the needs and concerns of others, deal with others tactfully, and work effectively with others in both routine and emotionally stressful situations
- Recognize and appreciate special needs and multicultural sensitivities and differences; relate well with others regardless of their backgrounds or personally held values
- Know what to say and what not to say in particular situations, send effective verbal and nonverbal messages, and accurately interpret nonverbal messages sent by others
- Match verbal style to others in a group

What Is Effective Communication?

Effective leaders demonstrate effective communication when they

- Articulate beliefs and defend decisions persuasively; communicate so that the intended messages are received and understood by targeted audiences
- Format communications effectively; adapt speech and presentations to specifically reach different audiences
- Monitor the "grapevine" and take action to dispel negative rumors and correct misinformation
- Practice effective listening skills and accurately interpret real messages being sent before responding
- Interact frequently with internal and external opinion leaders; actively work to develop common perceptions about issues
- Respond skillfully to news media; initiate and report news
- Recognize that many leader communications are aimed at marketing; tailor communications to appeal to the interests of different market segments
- Identify and adopt the behavior necessary to inspire others or that the particular audience expects, enabling them to assume the appropriate role that will best promote a preplanned response or action from followers

How's Your Demeanor/Deportment Quotient?

We've examined the three identified leader competencies—conceptual, anthropological, and technical—in terms of both requisite operative leader abilities and methods of delivery as evidenced in specific leader behaviors. Now, we need to consider how such competencies, abilities, and behaviors *are modified or enhanced by personal qualities.* Let's call these personal qualities *demeanor* and *deportment.* Demeanor is the manner in which you present yourself, the way in which you outwardly manifest your personality or attitude, and your style and essence of communication (especially verbal). Demeanor includes your characteristic posture and your customary ways of moving and gesturing when addressing others. For the purpose of this discussion, define deportment as your actions, manners, behaviors, and conduct primarily molded by your upbringing or training.

So now, to round out this picture of your potential effectiveness as a leader—the picture that you'd like others to have of you—it's expected that you will demonstrate positive demeanor and the kind of deportment that supports your position. Prospective followers expect that you will

- Exhibit personal and professional conduct, bearing, and appearance that conform to the conventions, proprieties, and mores of the enterprise and the greater community
- Use words and gestures, exemplify attitudes, and act in ways that are consistent with a genuine respect for the rights and dignity of others
- Model the desirable leadership qualities of integrity, self-respect, self-confidence, vision, patience, perseverance, and courage
- Act in a consistent and ethical manner

What Is This Thing Called Charisma?

Discussions of leadership theory frequently identify *charisma* as a powerful leadership trait, and we'd be remiss if we didn't consider this ability to capture imagination, as well as mind, at this point. Weber borrowed the term charisma, according to Freund, from Rudolph Sohm, a Strasbourg church jurist and historian (Freund, 1968; Weber, 1945). The term literally means "gift of grace." The idea of charisma is value-free and equally applicable to the "bad"person as it is to the "good" person. ("With her charisma, she could sell a skateboard to my 87-year-old grandmother." *or* "He had all the charisma in the world, but he couldn't lead or manage worth diddly!")

Charismatic qualities are measured not so much by their intrinsic power as by the nature and intensity of the devotion that some following attributes to them. People will identify your charisma not by the substantive character of what you say or do but by the supra-national, supra-utilitarian attachment of followers (Nisbet, 1996). Without measurable, seeable, doable actions, however, your so-called charisma will only persist in fleeting moments of its existence.

Without actions, charisma has little chance of surviving and becoming a part of the followers' perception or aggregate impression of leadership—unless of course, followers continue to attribute your primary leadership skills to the "gift of grace." In other words—no action, no long-lasting followers. And if you think you have some gift of grace—some supra-utilitarian power that will sustain your long-term efforts—bottle and market it immediately. I'll buy some!

NOW, LET'S TALK AGGREGATE IMPRESSION

So far you've looked at (a) the three leader competencies: conceptual, anthropological, and technical, which have been defined by (b) requisite operative leader abilities and demonstrated in (c) sample behaviors. And you understand that (a), (b), and (c), above, are modified or enhanced by the personal qualities designated as demeanor and deportment. Now, no more bullets, just the very important synthesis of these bullets into *your* act. You've dutifully followed enough typographical bullets to support the overthrow of a small country, and at this point you need to move ahead, of course assuming that you've mastered all of the competencies already explained. What you've really mastered is now going to be measured entirely by followers' *aggregate impression* of you, an impression that is developed and modified over time. We need now to take a close look at what constitutes others' aggregate impression of you. Have you provided them with the kinds of impressions over time that would lead them to believe they'd like to follow you?

Because the way people perceive you is likely to influence their interpretation of your behavior and the course of your future interactions with them, understanding the person perception process is central to the development of your leadership profile. Here's an overview of that process.

General Impression. When we meet you for the first time, we begin to form a *general impression* almost immediately. Although such a general impression may be inaccurate, we develop a sense of whether we like or dislike you and what are your personality and traits. "Wow, he has charisma!" "I fell in love with her at first sight!"

"I knew right away that we could work together." This is the starting point of our aggregate impression of you.

The cognitive process involved in the acquisition of information
about you, and in making judgments about you, is identified by
social psychologists as a person's information-processing approach.
For example, when we first meet you, our initial reactions are based
on whatever fragmentary information is available about you. This
information may be based on hearsay, reputation, or documented
history or limited to physical or social characteristics, for example,
you're tall, attractive, well-dressed, well-spoken.

Although our initial reactions to you often don't possess the
degree of certainty reflected in the statements above, we develop
general impressions of you with remarkable ease and speed. In addition, our initial reactions are often augmented by inferences concerning what else about you is likely to be true. These inferences are
frequently based on stimuli such as those listed previously under
Demeanor/Deportment, as well as physical attractiveness, gender,
race, age, and so on. This evaluative bias, or *halo effect*, occurs normally in inference processes. So, the question you need to ask yourself at this point is, what do others infer about me?

Primary Impression. If we meet or observe you only once, we may
never develop an impression beyond the initial general one. When
we expect to interact with you over time, however, we want as much
information about you as possible. We immediately begin to augment our general impression by making inferences about *what else* is
likely to be true about you. These are called *primary impressions* and
this phenomenon occurs regularly in the person perception process.
Whether such inferences are valid or invalid is irrelevant at this
point in the process. Our inferences are "true" for us and will have
an important bearing on our immediate perceptions of you.

As we get to know you better, we acquire more information
(e.g., style of interaction, free time interests, aspirations, concerns),
as well as perceive strengths and weaknesses or insecurities. With
the acquisition of new information about you, we develop primary
impressions that modify or elaborate our general perception of what
you are like and that can influence judgments we make about you.
Your next question might be, am I building a positive primary impression that will strengthen or modify others' general impression
of me?

Secondary Impression. When you work with us or encounter us on multiple occasions, over time we continue to modify our perceptions based on our observations of your behavior or actions in different circumstances. To the extent that those actions confirm our expectations, they reinforce our primary impression. To the extent that your actions contradict our expectations, we add the new impressions to our initial perception. We gain a better, fuller picture of who you are and what we can expect from you in the future. These are *secondary impressions.* Our secondary impressions help us make decisions about whether we like you, are comfortable in your presence, and would like to get to know you even better.

Tertiary Impression. Our third-level impressions, *tertiary impressions,* are closely tied to our personal value systems and are key to our decisions to trust, make a commitment to, or follow you. We form these tertiary impressions when we observe your behaviors toward others we care about or actions in situations that are value laden for us or in which we have a vested interest. To the extent that you share our value system and act or behave in a manner we approve, our impression of you is enhanced. To the extent that we are disappointed in your behavior or actions, our impression of you becomes more negative.

Aggregate Impression. Through ongoing observations of you, we form, supplement, interpret, and categorize our impressions in different ways. In doing so, we develop an *aggregate impression* that influences all of our perceptions of, and interactions with, you. Each new piece of information we receive reinforces or modifies our aggregate impressions. Our aggregate impression of you is, therefore, not a fixed or rigid perception, but one that is dynamic and subject to change over time. It can be very positive one day, negative the next, then positive again—depending on the behavior or actions we observe and the circumstances that surround them.

Although we form aggregate impressions about everyone with whom we interact on a regular basis, the central concern of this chapter is the aggregate impression of you in a leadership role. Figure 6.1 illustrates a continuum of aggregate impression as varying perceptions of leadership held by others (superiors, peers, subordinates, patrons/customers, etc.).

102

Figure 6.1.

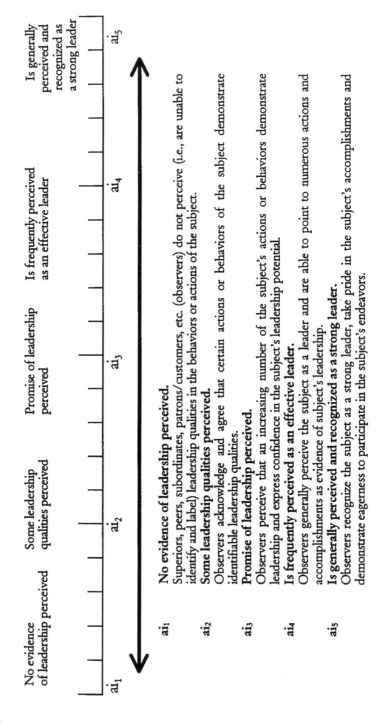

No evidence of leadership perceived	Some leadership qualities perceived	Promise of leadership perceived	Is frequently perceived as an effective leader	Is generally perceived and recognized as a strong leader
ai_1	ai_2	ai_3	ai_4	ai_5

ai_1 **No evidence of leadership perceived.**
Superiors, peers, subordinates, patrons/customers, etc. (observers) do not perceive (i.e., are unable to identify and label) leadership qualities in the behaviors or actions of the subject.

ai_2 **Some leadership qualities perceived.**
Observers acknowledge and agree that certain actions or behaviors of the subject demonstrate identifiable leadership qualities.

ai_3 **Promise of leadership perceived.**
Observers perceive that an increasing number of the subject's actions or behaviors demonstrate leadership and express confidence in the subject's leadership potential.

ai_4 **Is frequently perceived as an effective leader.**
Observers generally perceive the subject as a leader and are able to point to numerous actions and accomplishments as evidence of subject's leadership.

ai_5 **Is generally perceived and recognized as a strong leader.**
Observers recognize the subject as a strong leader, take pride in the subject's accomplishments and demonstrate eagerness to participate in the subject's endeavors.

We began with the assumptions that (a) regardless of the knowledge and skills, competencies and behavior a prospective leader may exhibit, leadership is possible only when other people (i.e., followers) grant the power necessary to lead; and (b) people grant leader status to another based on their perceptions of who the leader candidate is, what he or she stands for (shared values and beliefs), and the degree to which he or she can be trusted to speak or act effectively on their behalf. If we accept these assumptions, then we might also assume that for you to be granted leader status, the aggregate impressions of the you that the followers have must fit somewhere on the right-hand side of the continuum in Figure 6.1.

MANAGEMENT OF OTHERS' PERCEPTIONS (AGGREGATE IMPRESSION) THROUGH ROLE ASSUMPTION

An important corollary to the concept of aggregate impression is based on the additional assumptions that (a) followers develop their perceptions over time as people observe and interpret your behaviors and actions in a variety of situations and circumstances; and (b) if you are continuously aware of the perception development process, then you can consciously reinforce your aggregate impression as a leader in the eyes of your followers. The corollary is that as a prospective leader, you can actively manage other people's perceptions (aggregate impressions) of your leadership abilities by presenting yourself to others, through the behaviors you exhibit and the roles you play, in ways that reinforce your leader status. Many of the items listed under leader competencies, behaviors, and demeanor emphasize the importance of your ability to communicate with diverse groups with equal effectiveness. In reality, this means assuming different roles as circumstances dictate. Effective leaders, then, are by definition skilled actors.

Effective leaders assume a different role each time they modify their behavior to achieve some desired goal, get someone to do something, persuade someone of something, win trust or respect. In various circumstances and in our various relationships, we all pursue our needs by behaving in certain ways. And as is true in the theater, each role has its own appropriate behavior, speech, thought, and feelings, and each situation has its own character demands

(Benedetti, 1990). "As an actor [leader], you are a pleader of causes. The characters you play have a cause, a purpose, and it is up to you to plead it with utmost integrity and commitment" (Danson, cited in Benedetti, 1990, p. xii).

Role assumption should never be viewed by others as an act. Followers must continue to perceive your actions as genuine rather than manipulative. For example, Michael Chekhov is recognized as one of the most extraordinary actors and teachers of the 20th century. Chekhov, according to critics, was able to step outside of himself to comply with each character's demands. They questioned whether what Chekhov did on the stage was actually acting and noted, "It was as if the real characters from the pages of Shakespeare, Gogol, Dickens, Dostoyevsky, and Strindberg had mysteriously dropped down to earth, momentarily interacting with other performers" (Gordon, cited in Chekhov, 1991, p. ix).

Comparing the identified competencies, abilities, sample behaviors, and personal qualities described as demeanor/deportment with some of the "actors tools" presented in Table 6.1, we can see similarities between the methods used by successful actors and those used by effective leaders.

Just as the actor is both limited and empowered by actions, so too the effective leader can only express by action. A leader's language is a language of movement, of gesture, of voice, of the creation and projection of character. You don't need to become a professional actor, but the ability to assume different roles while maintaining integrity, and to shift from role to role smoothly, creates a powerful foundation for developing and maintaining an aggregate impression as a leader.

THE BOTTOM LINE

Schools and school districts continue to face unprecedented challenges. If survival is the watchword, then leadership is the key. Theories of leadership abound, and as in other social sciences, no strategy or theory is ever completely replaced. The hypotheses presented here (a synopsis of which can be found in Note 2) complement existing theories by identifying competencies and behaviors that distinguish leaders from managers, further reinforcing one

Table 6.1

Actor's Tools	Leader's Tools
The preparation of self	Understanding self
Limbering and aligning	Posture and presence
Gesture	Posture/presence as communication
Voice, diction, rhythm	Dynamics
Speech	Sound and projection
Working with others	Relationship, commitment, teamwork
The performance environment	Playing the room
The flow of action	Choice and character, toward an objective
Emotion	Assuming the correct role
Text analysis	Role of analytical thinking— right- and left-brain functions
Imagery and figurative language	Using the senses
Attitude	Desire for success and fear of failure

SOURCE: Adapted from Benedetti (1990, p. ix).

early theory of leadership that suggests simply that the leader is the one who succeeds in getting others to follow (Cowley, 1928). The theory of aggregate impression leadership adds that leaders lead through the power of influence, rather than the influence of power, and describes how leadership can be developed and maintained over time.

Now, you need to understand how this theory works for you; what adjustments, if any, you need to make in your behaviors; and whether or not you have the capabilities to influence others, act like, or be, a leader—ultimately an effective principal/leader.

NOTES

1. Why develop theory rather than examine practice? I believe that practice creates theory, and Chapter 5 includes the results of

effective practice as observed by numerous researchers over many years. Unlike earlier leadership research, however, this current chapter combines the findings of leadership researchers and practitioners with the findings and observations of scholars and practitioners from other domains. It examines the person rather than the purpose, affect rather than effect, and suggests a new hypothesis that demonstrates pure leadership in both normative and summative form. Readers should consider the theory presented in this chapter as provisional in nature and examine it on a deductive-inductive continuum and as a whole rather than in parts. Science has been defined as the enterprise by which a particular kind of ordered knowledge is obtained about natural phenomena by means of controlled observations and theoretical interpretation. At this maximal point, interpretation/explanation becomes theory: a patterning of logical constructs into which the known facts regarding a theoretical domain may be fitted. Science assumes that events are determined, that cause exists. The theory with which this chapter is concerned is one that can be tested through research studies and is, therefore, scientific in nature. In addition, my goal is to present a hypothesis that will meet the usually accepted goals of scientific effort and increase understanding, permit prediction, and facilitate influence. See Marx (1963); see also Dubin (1969).

2. *Foundational Hypothesis:* An absolute analysis of leadership *theory* should be void of management skills. An absolute analysis of leadership *practice* should be limited to three discernible competencies: conceptual, anthropological, and technical.

Basic Formula I: $L = C + A + T$

where L designates **leadership** *and where* (C), (A), and (T) are leader **competencies,** i.e., Conceptual, Anthropological, and Technical, respectively.

Developmental Hypothesis I: The three identified leader competencies—conceptual **(C)**, anthropological **(A)**, and technical **(T)**—are defined by requisite operative leader abilities. Subscripts **(a)** indicate the *requisite operative leader abilities* (e.g., ability to: see, understand, perceive, etc.).

Basic Formula II: $L = C_a + A_a + T_a$

Developmental Hypothesis II: The three identified leader competencies—conceptual **(C)**, anthropological **(A)**, and technical **(T)**— defined by the requisite operative leader abilities **(a)**, are further defined by methods of delivery or *specific leader behaviors* **(b)**. Examples of leader behaviors are described under the headings of executive leadership, problem solving/decision making/judgment, sensitivity, and communication.

Basic Formula III: $L = C_{ab} + A_{ab} + T_{ab}$

where **(b)** designates specific leader *behaviors* that illustrate the identified leader abilities and overall competencies.

Developmental Hypothesis III: The three identified leader competencies—conceptual **(C)**, anthropological **(A)**, and technical **(T)**defined by the requisite operative leader abilities **(a)** and sample behaviors **(b)**, are modified or enhanced by *personal qualities designated as demeanor/deportment* **(D)**.

Basic Formula IV: $L = C_{ab} + A_{ab} + T_{ab} + D$

where **(D)** designates examples of appropriate ***demeanor/deportment.***

Concluding Hypothesis: The three identified leader competencies—conceptual **(C)**, anthropological **(A)**, and technical **(T)**—defined by the requisite operative leader abilities **(a)** and sample behaviors **(b)** and modified or enhanced by personal qualities designated as demeanor/deportment **(D)** are finally defined by follower impressions that are enhanced and tempered over time. Consequently, leadership is dependent on the follower's *aggregate impression (AI)* of a leader's competencies, abilities, behaviors, and demeanor/deportment over an unspecified span of time[t].

Concluding Formula: $L = (C_{ab} + A_{ab} + T_{ab} + D)(AI^t)$

*where **(AI)** designates **aggregate impression** and **(t)** designates an unspecified span of time.*

3. *Operative:* Functioning effectively, efficiently.

4. *Position power:* Those who occupy official positions in the hierarchy of an organization exercise vested authority, which is the legitimate right to command. Legal authority for forcible domination and coercion—i.e., reward power, coercive power, legitimate power.

5. *Leadership power:* Expert power, referent power/personal charisma, or ideas so admired by others that they are induced by the opportunity not only to be associated with the power holder (power vested by followers), but also, insofar as possible, to become more like him or her.

6. *Authenticity:* Acts in ways that are consistently perceived to be truthful, genuine, reality based. Takes responsibility for choices. Is credible in any chosen role (e.g., sensitive, demanding, etc.).

7. *Leader behaviors:* Additional examples can be generated. Care must be taken, however, to ensure that any additions are *not* management skills and do *not* describe management behaviors.

REFERENCES

Benedetti, R. L. (1990). *The actor at work.* Englewood Cliffs, NJ: Prentice Hall.

Bennis, W., & Namus, B. (1998). *Leaders: The strategies for taking charge.* New York: Harper & Row.

Burns, J. M. (1985). *Leadership.* New York: Harper & Row.

Chekhov, M. (1991). *On the technique of acting.* New York: HarperCollins.

Cowley, W. H. (1928, April). Three distinctions in the study of leaders. *Journal of Abnormal and Social Psychology,* pp. 144-157.

Dubin, R. (1969). *Theory building.* New York: Free Press.

Freund, J. (1968). *The sociology of Max Weber.* New York: Pantheon.

Getzels, J. W., Lipham, J., & Campbell, R. (1968). *Educational administration as a social process.* New York: Harper & Row.

Lipham, J. M. (1964). Leadership and administration. In D. Griffins (Ed.), *Behavioral science and educational administration* (63rd yearbook of the National Society for the Study of Education. Chicago: University of Chicago Press.

Marx, M. (1963). *Theories in contemporary psychology.* New York: Macmillan.

Nisbet, R. (1996). *The sociological tradition.* New York: Basic Books.

Owens, R. G. (1998). *Organizational behavior in education* (6th ed.). Needham Heights, MA: Allyn & Bacon.

Rothlisberger, F. J. (1968). *Man in organization.* Cambridge, MA: Harvard University Press.

Schmidt, W. H., & Finnegan, J. P. (1992). *The race without a finish line: America's quest for total quality.* San Francisco: Jossey-Bass.

Sherif, M. (1967). *Social interaction.* Chicago: Aldine.

Weber, M. (1945). *The theory of social and economic organization.* (T. Parsons, Ed.; A. Henderson & T. Parsons, Trans.). New York: Oxford University Press.

7

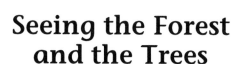

Seeing the Forest
and the Trees

*Blending the Best of Management
and Leadership*

ABOUT THIS CHAPTER

Previously, we talked about leadership as being separate from management, and we explored the concept of leadership in Chapter 6. Now, we need to explore the idea of management. It's important to understand—and remember—that although leadership and management behaviors often overlap, leadership is something earned over time, something you build on, with power bestowed by *followers*. A manager, on the other hand, exercises power bestowed by *superiors* and is usually limited to responsibilities and accountabilities for resources. Effective managers may also be leaders, and most leaders practice effective management techniques. But the two roles involve unique behaviors (Shafritz & Russell, 1997). This chapter is limited to the distinct behaviors, functions, and tasks of management in the school culture.

> In 1997, reports the Labor Department, there were 18 million executives, managers and administrators in the United States. I am not one of them. No one works for me or is supervised by me . . . no one has ever hinted that I deserved greater power and responsibility. Perish the thought.

All this may explain why I have a certain grudging respect for managers. I am obviously unfit to do whatever it is they do. They seem to relish responsibility while I dread it. They have, or feign, confidence, while I shudder at putting a subject and verb in every sentence. What baffles me is why people want to be managers. Granted some rewards are tempting: power, money, status and (possibly) the respect of co-workers. But the drawbacks seem as plain: resentment from below, pressure from above, loud criticism of failures, silence over successes. No thanks.

. . . The almost universal task of managers today, in our culture, is to serve twin masters, each of whom has grown more demanding. There's the organization, with its imperatives; and there's the Individual, each with "needs." This is a tough job, and somebody's got to do it. But not me. (Samuelson, 1999, p. A21)

REFLECTIVE POINT

Management as defined in this chapter is based on three interrelated assumptions:

1. There are identifiable competencies and behaviors that will distinguish you as an effective manager, separate from the competencies that will distinguish you as an effective leader.

2. *Strategic* goals are developed by leaders. Managers provide *tactical* responses to strategic goals.

3. Effective principals exhibit the strongest traits of both leadership and management behavior.

HOW MANAGERS MANAGE

Style Alignment

Clearly, we expect you to be a leader in your role as principal. You're going to spend a great deal of your time managing, however.

Let's assume that you're easily able to manage the day-to-day operations of your school—students, parents, teachers, facilities, the lunch program, buses, and so on—certainly a big job. But there's a still bigger job: managing in such a way that your superiors—*your* leaders, your bosses—see your management style as being compatible with *their* style.

What your bosses need from you is assurance that their role, whatever it is, remains strong. You can provide this assurance by making sure you understand your superiors' modus operandi and the environment in which they work. For example, you have to understand your superiors' goals and objectives; professional pressures; and individual strengths, weaknesses, blind spots, and preferred work styles. At the same time you have to continuously assess your needs, your own strengths and weaknesses, your personal style, and your predisposition toward autonomy from authority figures. Understanding both your superiors' and your own modus operandi will help you develop and maintain a relationship that fits *mutual* needs and styles; is characterized by shared expectations; allows for ease of communications; is based on dependability and honesty; and, most important, uses your superiors' time and resources wisely (Gabarro & Kotter, 1987).

Now, you may resent the fact that in addition to all your other responsibilities you also need to take time and energy to manage your relationship with bosses. Effective principals recognize, however, that relationship management is a necessary and critical part of their overall management tasks. They know they need to establish and manage alliances with everyone on whom they are in any way dependent.

Okay, with this in mind, let's move on and identify those attributes that separate your management tasks from your leadership initiatives. Building on Chapter 6, where we examined leadership from the perspective of behaviors that affect change, set direction, and align and motivate people, let's examine specific management behaviors—those behaviors that are the *tactical* tools you need to use to effect the implementation of your *strategic* leadership goals. Your leadership behavior has allowed you to develop strategic plans and to motivate followers to implement such plans. Now, you change your hat from leader to manager so you can develop tactical responses to your own leadership strategies and *direct* people to a desired outcome. As leader, you've set the stage; now, as manager, push the furniture in place. As manager, you will harness organizational complexity while you plan and budget and organize and supervise necessary personnel on the job. Please remember, however, that although management complements leadership, it doesn't replace it. As stated earlier, in the ideal world, an effective leader would also be an effective manager. In your job as an effective principal, you will be expected to provide that "ideal world" and exhibit the strongest traits of both effective leadership and effective management.

To recall the leadership behaviors outlined in the previous chapter, here are some examples of managerial behavior.

Responsibility Functions

First, in the area of responsibility, the principal assumes the following management functions:

Plans	Organizes
Identifies desired results	Prioritizes tasks
Identifies tasks	Sequences tasks
Identifies resources and tools	Develops work schedules
	Calculates time needed
	Assembles resources and tools

Coordinates	Communicates
Supervises the completion of tasks	Directions
	Process
Monitors work in progress	Activities
Adjusts activities or schedule	Use of resources
	Timelines
	Expectations
	Specific results
	Priorities

Program Management Functions

Second, building on the functions listed above, the effective principal acts as a program manager who

- Plans, organizes, and directs the work of faculty and staff; makes assignments and develops schedules that promote the most efficient and effective use of human resources; practices effective time management

- Interprets, enforces, and administers school district policies and procedures in a consistent manner; develops, communicates, and implements comprehensive school policies and procedures for faculty, staff, and student personnel to promote a positive learning environment and safeguard the physical and emotional well-being of all

- Puts programs and plans into action; applies appropriate management techniques (e.g., facilitates tasks, establishes progress checkpoints, considers alternative approaches, provides midcourse corrections when appropriate) to bring about organizational change; adapts quickly and effectively to new conditions

- Applies accepted principles of growth and development and teaching and learning to develop a curricular and co-curricular program that accommodates differences in cognition and achievement and promotes student progress

- Directs individuals or groups to develop education programs and promote a positive teaching/learning environment; evaluates teaching methods and strategies to ensure appropriateness

- Monitors school district curricula; works with faculty, community, and central office to plan and implement a framework for instruction; initiates needs analyses and monitors social and technological developments that affect curricula; recommends changes in curricular content as needs and conditions change

- Uses a variety of techniques and strategies to assess the achievement of curricular goals and the effectiveness of the total instructional program; determines the extent to which outcomes meet or exceed previously defined standards, goals, or priorities; draws inferences for program revision; seeks and encourages input from a variety of sources to improve the school's program

- Demonstrates understanding of school budgets (general and activity); conducts a systematic process to involve faculty, staff, and the community in developing budget priorities; plans, prepares, justifies, and defends the school budget and manages the school within that budget

- Ensures that accurate personnel, pupil, and financial records are kept and reported as required; processes purchase orders, work orders, and other school business transactions accurately and in a timely manner; audits accounts regularly

People Management Functions

Third, building on the identified functions along with the principal's role as a program manager, the principal acts as a people manager who

- Uses a variety of techniques to assess performance; examines the extent to which performance meets or exceeds previously defined standards or goals for individuals or groups; interprets measurements or evaluations for others
- Provides for guidance, counseling, and ancillary services; responds to family needs; enlists the participation of appropriate individuals and groups to design and conduct programs that create relevant links between school activities and plans for adult life; plans and implements a comprehensive program of student activities
- Develops realistic performance plans with faculty and staff; clarifies expectations and holds faculty and staff responsible for timely and effective completion of assignments
- Provides faculty and staff with regular feedback on performance strengths and weaknesses in a constructive manner to sustain or improve performance and conducts formal performance reviews in a direct, thorough, and timely manner, based on documented performance
- Takes effective action to hire faculty and staff or remove poorly performing employees in accordance with district policies and procedures
- Recognizes personnel problems and develops plans to resolve them in a timely manner; uses discretion in addressing, discussing, and documenting personnel problems
- Identifies the professional development needs of individuals and groups; plans, organizes, and implements programs to improve faculty and staff effectiveness

The Evolution of Administration

Although the words *management, leadership,* and *administration* are often used interchangeably, you can see by comparing Chapter 6 with this chapter that they have different meanings. In simple terms,

- *Leadership* focuses on determining organizational objectives and strategies, building consensus for meeting those objectives, and influencing others to work toward the objectives. Leadership deals with the top line: What are the things I want to accomplish?
- *Management* is a process of developing tactical plans to implement strategies and control resources in an effort to achieve organizational objectives. Management has a bottom-line focus: How can I accomplish certain things?

And just to confuse things,

- *Administration* has a broader meaning in the education enterprise, one that encompasses both management and leadership (Kowalski & Reitzug, 1993): What do I want to accomplish *and* how can I do it?

So, your job as a principal really calls for you to have an effective combination of both leadership abilities and management responsibilities packaged in a neat bundle called school administration. Okay, Administrator—here, *in very general terms,* is your *real* job description.

You will, in your administrative/leadership role,

Lead Change and Understand	**Build a Power Base**
The process of change	Internal
The pressures for change	External
The resistance to change	District
Understand Types of Influence	**Build Coalitions**
Motivate, Innovate, Foster Creativity	**Take Calculated Risks**

You will, in your *administrative/managerial* role,

Manage Human Resources

Staff
  Selection
  Motivation
  Mentoring
  Evaluation
  Discipline
Faculty
  Selection
  Motivation
  Mentoring
  Evaluation
  Discipline
  Union activity
  Negotiated constraints and
    obligations
  Middle-management role
Student
  Motivation
  Mentoring
  Evaluation
  Discipline
  Special needs
Parents and patrons
  Motivation
  Mentoring
  Special needs
District administrators
Board of education

Manage Communications

Communication styles
Listening
Intraschool, interschool, and
  district
School-community relations and
  marketing

Manage Physical Resources

Plant
Grounds
Supplies
Equipment

Manage Environments

Security
Contingency planning
Safety

Manage Technology

Equitable access and distribution
Instructional applications
Administrative applications
Communication applications
Maintenance of hardware
Technical assistance

Manage Curriculum

Mandated and nonmandated
Activities
Censorship

Manage Fiscal Resources

Budget input
Activity funds
General funds

Manage Problems

Decision making
Conflict
Risk and litigation
Crisis avoidance

The preceding thumbnail sketch demonstrates what the daily
leadership and management activities of school-based administrators (also known as principals) look like. There's more—pages and

pages more, but that's an encyclopedia of information best learned on the job. The preceding outline clearly illustrates how you can easily be caught up in a management paradigm, however—how easily managerial functions and task resolution can overpower your role as leader. But this we know for a fact: Effective management without effective leadership is, as someone phrased it, "like straightening deck chairs on the Titanic." No management success can compensate for failure in leadership.

THE BOTTOM LINE

Don't apply for this job!

Wanted: School Administrator who pushes people in the right direction without the constant need to motivate them by satisfying basic human needs. A person who is capable of simply shaping the work environment, crafting tactical plans, marshaling resources, and developing star performers. Special consideration will be given to the candidate who is experienced in organizational body building, is disciplined in command and control, and easily adapts to zero-tolerance mandates.

Do apply for this job!

Wanted: School Administrator. The School District of Lancaster has an immediate opening for a principal. Beyond the prerequisite certification, we are looking for a dynamic individual—a bright, motivated professional:

- Who believes that decisions that impact the effectiveness of individual schools should be made at the school level.
- Who understands the importance of teamwork and is willing to partner with teachers, administrators, staff, and the community as stakeholders in the future of children.
- Who understands what it means to lead a standards-based, results-oriented school.
- Who has energy, enthusiasm, and a belief in one's self as an educator and life-long learner.

- Who is creative, open to new ideas, and willing to test different approaches.
- Who is willing to be a pioneer and agent for positive change in public education.

We are seeking a smart, savvy, strategic individual who knows how to build instructional excellence within a school as well as manage day-to-day operations. (*Education Week,* 1999, p. 51)

At the beginning of this chapter you read that leadership strategizes actions and motivates people, while management develops tactical responses to leadership strategies and directs people to a desired outcome. Managers harness organizational complexity, plan and budget, and organize and supervise necessary personnel on the job. And you read, "Management complements leadership; it doesn't replace it." You also read, "In the ideal world, an effective leader would also be an effective manager. In your job as an effective principal, you'll be expected to provide that 'ideal world' and exhibit the strongest traits of both effective leadership and effective management."

You should be prepared to work and succeed in an "ideal world" culture. It's a challenge, I know, but just think of this: You'll never have the time to get bored, much less the time to figure out, really, whether you're managing or leading at any given point. That's an ironic statement, isn't it?—considering that we have spent two chapters differentiating between the unique competencies and behaviors of leadership versus those of management. Well, in practice you don't really need to be aware of whether you are leading or managing in any particular situation. What matters is that you *act* in the appropriate role, at the appropriate time. And that you *act effectively*, using basic savvy and smart guessing to arrive at the best action given the circumstances. And what's your reward for effectively juggling leadership and management roles at the end of the day? The aggregate impression of you that your followers—and your superiors—hold will be stronger than it was the previous day.

REFERENCES

Gabarro, J., & Kotter, J. (1987). Managing your boss. In *People: Managing your most important asset* (pp. 7-9). Cambridge, MA: Harvard Business Review.

Kowalski, T. J., & Reitzug, U. C. (1993). *Contemporary school administration: An introduction.* New York: Longman.

Samuelson, R. J. (1999, March 18). Why I am not a manager. *Washington Post*, p. A21.

Shafritz, J. M., & Russell, E. W. (1997). *Introducing public administration.* New York: Longman.

Education Week. (1999, April 7). [Advertisement by school district of Lancaster, PA]. p. 51.

8

Let's Meet, So You
Can "Ooh" and "Aah"
Over My Experience

Marketing Campaigns and Initiation Rituals

ABOUT THIS CHAPTER

If you're a preservice/potential principal reading this book, then by now you've either decided that the principalship is "the ship of fools"—or declared that you are ready to launch your own principalship. We hope the latter. If you're currently serving in a quasi-administrative position or in a vice principalship and are hoping to move into your own principalship, sail full speed ahead! This chapter is about the eye-opening and treacherous rituals that often take place between the time you apply for a principal position and the time you actually land one. If you're currently in a principalship and want to move to another school or another position,

---

AUTHOR'S NOTE: The research and writing for this chapter were done entirely by Janet Mendis, a doctoral candidate in Education Leadership at George Mason University and an education consultant. Mendis has served on more than a half dozen community interview panels representing parent and special education perspectives in selecting principals and assistant superintendents in two large school districts and in her capacity as a professional writer/editor has assisted numerous job hunters in crafting their résumés.

then this chapter is also for you. Regardless of your eventual destination, the reality is that you need to market yourself successfully to your prospective "buyers."

There's more to marketing yourself than checking your makeup or straightening your tie every 10 minutes. To "sell" yourself, you need to master a new way of thinking—learn to think strategically, statistically, and creatively. Such thinking is not something you can master overnight. Rather, it is a heightened awareness you develop over time through your understanding of your school district's culture, through your deeds and accomplishments, and through an awareness of who you are and where you want to be. Personal awareness enables you to turn a new lens on yourself.

This chapter is designed to help you see yourself as a marketable commodity, no more and no less than a cut of beef. The trick, of course, is to sell yourself as a must-have filet mignon! The chapter also outlines some of the challenges you will encounter en route to your goal, perhaps selection as principal (or assistant principal, for starters) to lead and manage a school. Or perhaps as a currently practicing principal, you're ready for new challenges at a different school or want to change your sphere of influence by tackling a district-level administrative position.

Because the preceding chapters have described a number of the artifacts and customs, spoken rules and unspoken codes, that constitute the culture of administration in both schools and school districts, you probably have some sense of the obvious as well as the hidden hazards. We've looked at the aggregate impression that you, as a prospective principal or a principal already in a school, need to cast in your followers' (and your bosses') minds. We know that if others see you as an effective leader, they will be inclined to follow your lead, and people in the central office will be inclined to give you the autonomy you will need to reach your goals.

We've looked at the numerous tasks and behaviors that competent managers demonstrate and noted that ideally an effective principal is a good leader *and* a good manager. The challenges of leading and managing effectively are formidable, and yet—you are still considering launching that principalship of your own. Maybe you believe you can do the job better than you've seen done or you know you can make a difference in more people's lives in that role. If you're a practicing principal already, maybe you're eager to test your mettle in a bigger arena. So, keeping to this book's sociological and cultural focus on schools and school leadership, let's examine the typical initiation rituals involved in choosing a principal.

> **ritual** *n* (1649) **1:** the established form for a ceremony; . . . **2a:** ritual observance; *specif:* a system of rites **b:** a ceremonial act or action **c:** any formal and customarily repeated act or series of acts (*Webster's Ninth New Collegiate Dictionary*, 1985, p. 1018)

This chapter provides "marketing" tips and advice, showing you how to structure your marketing documents so they support the aggregate impression of you as an effective leader. The chapter then places you in the middle of a principal selection process scenario that would have been unimaginable just a few years ago. Today, such scenarios occur regularly in school districts across the nation as

- The term *stakeholder* is used much more frequently in schools than in meat markets
- School board members can regularly be found telling superintendents to "get rid of" Principal So-and-So
- Parents count on legislators to address concerns about school safety and student achievement
- Students often become pawns in high-stakes budget deals and policy gambles

---

REFLECTIVE POINT

To present yourself as the best candidate for a principalship or any other administrative position, to be primed to show your strengths in the selection process, and to navigate the process with confidence and a healthy regard for your own self-protection, there are some steps to take. First, you need to get an interview, which entails creating a marketing package that sells your "goods" to those interested in "buying." Then, you better prepare yourself, if you want to not only survive the selection process but also succeed. Preparing yourself requires both mental preparation and fact-finding research. A principal selection process resembles initiation rituals that closed groups use in testing and admitting new members, so obtaining certain useful information in advance will help prepare you for the new game that lies ahead. In this chapter, you'll get an insider's glimpse at a prospective principal's experience with a community interview panel. If you're a veteran principal seeking to change schools or move to a district-level position, be forewarned that you too may be caught in a similar selection process game—if your marketing efforts are successful in moving you beyond the preliminary round (i.e., application). This chapter concludes with some reality-based advice on marketing yourself and succeeding at the selection process game.

The objective of this chapter is, then, to help you convince the world that you are the best person for the job. If you have the requisite qualifications, a strong performance record, a "rising star" aura, and recommendations from influential administrators (mentors), you just might be selected for further consideration and scrutiny from the pool of candidates. This chapter introduces you to—and prepares you for—the interview and selection process, which is the cultural "rite of passage" from one professional position to another.

SELLING YOURSELF AS "PRIME CUT"

So, Just What Makes You a Cut Above the Rest, Anyhow?

Confident, successful individuals know that their greatest competition is themselves and don't waste time worrying about other candidates for a desirable position, other bidders for a juicy contract, other suitors for a loved one's heart. "It is hard to fight an enemy who has outposts in your head" (Kempton, cited in *Quotable Women*, 1994, p. 44). If *you* are convinced that you have what it takes, you are already ahead in the game.

Believing in yourself is clearly the first step toward your goal. Now, you need to convince others—the diverse cast of characters involved in selecting a final candidate—that you are better than the rest. Your tool is the marketing package you create (i.e., your cover letter and résumé) to introduce yourself to those screening the applicants for the principalship. But before we get into specifics about how to market yourself, it's important to stop and think about what it is that makes you stand out above the rest. There are three basic areas in which you can distinguish yourself from others: what you know, what you can do, and who you are.

- *What You Know:* The knowledge you bring to the position includes that acquired through traditional higher education (e.g., graduate degrees, professional development activities) as well as that acquired through your experiences—and through your ability to learn from your experiences. The truth is that experiential wisdom and common sense are essential elements of any education leader's success, and in certain arenas such practical knowledge is valued more highly than university degrees and academic accomplishments. So, at a minimum, in your marketing package you need to list your graduate and undergraduate degrees as well as the professional certifications and endorsements you hold. If you are presently enrolled in coursework (e.g., on infusing Internet research skills into the curriculum) or have completed special district, state, or professional development training (e.g., in mediation and conflict resolution), then you will want to incorporate that information in your résumé.

- *What You Can Do:* Anyone with a realistic chance of being a serious candidate for a leadership position must have an established track record of significant professional accomplishments. Knowing what you can do is important, but you also will need to sell others on you as the unparalleled choice by identifying specific proven successes and contributions in your present and past positions and citing examples of times you have demonstrated particular skills. Remember that an administrative position is a leadership and management position. So highlight achievements that show evidence of your leadership and management abilities.

- *Who You Are:* Certainly, your own individual attributes and personal values also distinguish you from others.
  - *Individual Attributes:* The attributes that would label you as a cut above the others include such things as being a team player as well as being a calculated risk taker, a creative problem solver, an effective communicator, an ethical decision maker, and a careful listener.

♦ *Personal Values:* The personal beliefs that will make you stand out as a strong candidate are your views on such things as challenging students, faculty, and staff; developing critical thinkers as well as improving achievement test scores; and maintaining a safe school and a thriving learning environment.

Capturing Your Most Marketable Qualities on Paper

Clearly, you must be stellar in what you know, what you can do, and who you are. But to convince others of your stellarness, you need to capture that stellar self on paper, both in your cover letter and in your résumé. Even though you may have the requisite qualifications, an outstanding performance record, a "rising star" or even "meteoric" aura, and recommendations from the king and queen, you still need to play the selection process game.

Your cover letter should be intriguing enough to get any reader to turn to the next page—that is, your résumé. An impressive cover letter and résumé is your first opportunity to start building an aggregate impression of yourself as a leader in the minds of those involved in filling that principal slot—before they even meet you. A cover letter—your "door opener" if you write it right—is brief, respectful, and to the point. A maximum of two pages long, the cover letter says who you are, what position you seek, why you believe you are the best person for the job, and what you will bring to the job. Try to dovetail what you say about yourself with what the decision makers are looking for in filling a particular administrative position.

Now, probably someone has told you somewhere along the way that résumés should be only one page long. Although brevity in a résumé is critical, and thus only notable accomplishments should be included, if it takes two pages to present the important information that will sell you to your readers—then take the two pages. There are a number of equally effective formats you can use for your résumé, and libraries, and bookstores offer numerous how-to guides on writing and formatting résumés. To be consistent with this book's cultural perspective and insights, the following tips and advice focus specifically on how to market yourself in the administrative culture of a school district—not on how to format. So, regardless of which format you choose, pay careful attention to what you say, how you say it, and how it looks. Table 8.1 gives examples of what types of things to say about yourself and how to say them effectively if you're a teacher seeking an administrative position for the first time. Table 8.2 contains examples of how to present your "leader self" if you're already an administrator and are seeking another administrative position.

Table 8.1

Education

Example: Tell What You Know in Your Résumé

Ph.D., Education Leadership, George Mason University (1999)
Dissertation Topic: Changing the Special Education Service Delivery Model at the High School Level

M.Ed., Special Education, University of Illinois at Chicago (1990)
Areas of Specialization: Learning Disabilities, Behavior Disorders

B.A., English, University of Chicago (1985)

Virginia Certification: Supervision/Administration; English; Learning Disabilities

Illinois Type 10 Teaching Certificate, Learning Disabilities, K-12
Completed Illinois State Board of Education training in using mediation in conflict resolution

Relevant Experience and Professional Accomplishments

Example: Tell What You Can Do in Your Résumé

Chaired high school's task force of 23 special and general education teachers in developing departmental guidance and monthly workshops on adapting curriculum and teaching strategies for students with diverse learning needs. (1997–1999)

Organized network connecting high school faculty with those at its feeder schools (five elementary schools and one middle school) to facilitate regular dialogue regarding curriculum continuity and community-specific social and developmental issues. Program includes interschool teacher exchange visits, an annual half-day luncheon/retreat, and an Internet listserv for ongoing discussion. (1998–Present)

Example: Tell About Who You Are
(Your Individual Attributes) in Your Résumé

Developed and implemented high school's first "Local Heroes Essay
Contest," to focus attention on positive role models in the community,
to reinforce school's character education program efforts, and to
provide students with an opportunity to practice meaningful writing.
Panel of three judges selected 6 winners out of 30 entries, with cash
prizes of $100 awarded to winners. All entries published schoolwide;
some published in local newspaper. (1996–1997)

Example: Tell About Who You Are (Your Personal Values)
in Your Résumé

Established inclusion of high school Special Olympics athletes in the
school's seasonal award programs by working with the Athletic
Booster Club and the Athletic Director, with Special Olympians now
able to earn school letters for representing their school in local,
regional, and state competitions.

Table 8.2

Education

Example: Tell What You Know in Your Résumé

(The examples in Table 8.1 of how to state your education and any special
training or credentials are equally applicable for administrators looking to
change to another administrative position.)

Relevant Experience and Professional Accomplishments

Example: Tell What You Can Do in Your Résumé

Managed variety of school facilities, programs, budgets, and personnel as
building administrator for large metropolitan school district.
Recognized as district's most effective "change agent" and selected for
several critical "turn-around" assignments. Organizational results
included long-term cost reductions, and significant improvements in
accountability, test scores, student and adult personnel morale,
discipline, and attendance.

(continued)

Table 8.2 Continued

Elected president of district's principals association by peers and served two 2-year terms. Chaired association's district budget input committee (3 years), policy and regulations advisory task force (4 years), and special education service delivery improvement task force (2 years). Consistently called on to speak as association's representative on various topics to a range of audiences: school board members, legislators, local and regional PTAs and chambers of commerce, and civic groups.

Example: Tell About Who You Are (Your Individual Attributes) in Your Résumé

Developed district's mediation procedures, to become part of the conflict resolution process when parents of children with disabilities and school personnel disagree about placement decisions or services provided. Researched best practices. Developed materials for school personnel and parents to explain how mediation works and to equip them to participate in mediation as a nonadversarial route to determining what is best for students. Piloted program in high school and its feeder elementary and middle schools. Successfully resolved 80% of mediated disputes (i.e., issues resolved; no further due process appeals).

Example: Tell About Who You Are (Your Personal Values) in Your Résumé

Developed and implemented pilot expanded arts program for large diverse high school that extended current course offerings to include new dance classes (both classical and ethnic), multicultural music ensemble courses, and multimedia art classes (including culturally based art forms). Facilitated efforts of parents and community to expand curricular offerings that reflect the diverse student population and celebrate students' cultural heritages. Procured government and private sector funding to cover costs of implementing pilot program (e.g., personnel, curriculum development, course materials). Program widely supported by students (with 47% participating in at least one new course) and community (with 30 community members providing volunteer support) and served as a model for projects at three other high schools.

- *What You Say:* Your résumé should entice its readers to want to meet you in person. It should highlight your range of accomplishments, your breadth of experiences, and any special professional honors, recognition, awards you have earned. Remember that on this sheet of paper (or two), you need to present what you know, what you can do, and who you are in such a persuasive package that readers will see you as a very strong candidate. Whether you are seeking an initial or a different administrative position, obviously it's important to mention teaching and administrative accomplishments, but it's also extremely important to cite your professional activities outside the school. You're not trying to prove that you're an excellent teacher, vice principal, or principal (even though you undoubtedly are!). Instead, you're trying to sell yourself as someone who can see beyond the classroom walls, the school walls—someone who understands, and is capable of operating as a leader in, the administrative culture of the district. Notice in Table 8.1 that every example of telling who you are and what you can do describes an out-of-the-classroom leadership activity, and two of the four examples cite activities extending beyond one school. As a current administrator, you need to do the same to demonstrate that you also are able to see and work beyond the confines of your school. The examples in Table 8.2—presented here for current administrators who are seeking other positions—show the types of activities that demonstrate leadership. In both tables, you can see the leadership action verbs used to describe the person's role in each particular activity: "chaired . . . organized . . . developed and implemented . . . established . . . managed . . . recognized . . . elected . . . researched . . . piloted . . . resolved . . . facilitated . . . procured. . ."
- *How You Say It:* Select every word carefully. Don't waste words, or use mysterious acronyms, jargon, or dull (or flowery) language. Do use powerful vocabulary, descriptive nouns, and action verbs (such as those listed in Chapter 1 under the heading "When You're in Charge, Life Becomes an Action Verb"). When accomplishments can be best understood (or are more impressive) with quantitative measures,

by all means include such quantification. In the following example—*"Chaired county-wide task force of 35 secondary math teachers in examining and revising the algebra and geometry curricula in an intensive 4-week period (Summer 1999)"*—we know that this was a countywide leadership role, involving 35 teachers from different schools in a collaborative and comprehensive project over the course of 4 weeks.

- *How It Looks:* Although it's true that appearances aren't everything, it's also true that appearances convey an impression in the mind of the beholder that's hard to reverse. Appearance are part of a person's first impression of you. Many veteran personnel/human resource specialists simply trash résumés that contain spelling or grammatical errors. In such cases, the applicant never gets a second chance. You wouldn't go to an interview wearing a stained tie, a smelly shirt, or a hole in your hosiery, so don't send a sloppy résumé—the equivalent of dirty clothes—to introduce yourself to the decision makers. (Table 8.3, featuring excerpts from actual résumés, presents some unbelievable examples of résumé "dirty clothes.") Whatever format you decide to use, be sure that your résumé is attractive in its layout, impeccable in its spelling and punctuation, and organized in its presentation. Using parallel structure—for example, beginning each accomplishment with an action verb—helps the reader quickly comprehend your content. In these days of personal computers and laser printers, it is not necessary to get your résumé professionally printed to have your first "game piece" be an impressive paper representation of who you are.

WHAT *IS* THIS SELECTION PROCESS GAME YOU'VE BEEN INVITED TO PLAY?

The "New and Improved" Way Principals Are Chosen

In the olden days, superintendents (or their assistant superintendents, in larger districts) knew the up-and-coming leaders

Table 8.3

Making Weak Attempts at Humor

Don't try to be funny. You probably aren't.

"I have an excellent track record, although I am not a horse."

"Let's meet, so you can 'ooh' and 'aah' over my experience."

Baring Details Best Kept Deep Inside

Some things should remain unsaid. So, don't say them.

"Personal interests: Donating blood. Fourteen gallons so far."

"I have become completely paranoid, trusting completely no one and absolutely nothing."

"Marital status: Single. Unmarried. Unengaged. Uninvolved. No commitments."

"Marital status: Often. Children: Various."

Being a Bit Too Honest

Don't lie, but don't point out your worst faults or stupidest mistakes.

"Finished eighth in my class of ten."

"References: None. I've left a path of destruction behind me."

"I procrastinate, especially when the task is unpleasant."

"It's best for employers that I not work with people."

Forgetting to Proofread

A résumé is no place for Freud to slip.

"Reason for leaving last job: maturity leave."

"As indicted, I have over five years of analyzing investments."

"Instrumental in ruining entire operation for a Midwest chain store."

NOTE: Names and sources shall remain confidential to spare these unsuccessful applicants any further embarrassment.

among the district's teaching and administrative ranks. So, when a principal or other leadership position came open, the superintendent recommended someone for the job, the school board formally appointed the new administrator, and that was that. Nowadays, however, filling an administrative slot is rarely that simple.

Parent involvement in schools—frequently heralded as key to children's academic success, and in 1994 added to Congress's Goals 2000 list of national education goals—is a popular generic phrase that translates into a number of different assumptions and practices in school districts and individual schools. One area in which parents have become players—but sometimes under vague rules and with unclear roles—is in the domain of principal selection. In Chicago, part of the decentralization reform efforts instituted to improve the city's failing schools includes empowering parents in local community councils to essentially hire (and fire) principals, as well as allocate budgeted funds, and select curricula and teaching methods (Black, 1998). Even those of you who do not live in the Windy City will probably find parents involved in some manner when you venture into the principalship market.

We've already identified the various constituencies (besides the students) that you will need to please as principal of any school— parents, faculty, staff, area and central office personnel, school board members, business leaders, community leaders, and local politicians. Schools and school districts perform a delicate balancing act as they try to include parents and other stakeholders as partners while also seeking to keep that involvement from becoming interference (Black, 1998). Although few districts leave final hiring decisions up to community groups, you may face representatives of some or all of these constituencies on an interview panel charged with narrowing down the field of qualified candidates for a leadership position. Sometimes, stakeholders are invited to develop a list of priorities they would like the candidate to address, a list of personal qualifications they would like the candidate to possess, or a list of questions they would like all potential candidates to answer. Regardless of how your district chooses to involve the various interest groups, rest assured that the stakeholders will scrutinize you and all other candidates closely to see how you dance to the obstacles they throw in your path.

Assume Nothing About the Selection Process
Is as Simple as They Say

Consider this: A few years ago, a large suburban school district that usually includes a community interview panel as part of its principal selection process was seeking someone to succeed a popular high school principal who was retiring after 10 years at the school. The administrator conducting the selection process assured the finalists who faced the 12-member community panel that the panelists had agreed that interviews would be confidential and that everything discussed in the room would also be confidential. Copies of applicants' résumés were distributed 10 minutes before each applicant entered the room and were collected along with the panelists' rating sheets shortly after the conclusion of each interview. All applicants were asked the same nine questions developed by the school's faculty and parents prior to the interviews.

The panel consisted of three parents selected by the PTA (all PTA board members), three staff members (two teachers and the principal's secretary) selected by the staff, another high school principal, someone from the district's personnel office, the area director of special education, the area director of student services, the area director of elementary education, and a representative from the district's budget and finance office. The panelists were thanked for their willingness to participate in the selection process and were informed that their input and recommendations would be significant data that the area superintendent would consider in choosing the new principal. They were reminded that they were not the decision makers in the process, but as they were important community members, their views were valuable.

Eight of the finalists were internal applicants already working as assistant principals or principals in the district; two were principals in other districts. You can imagine the surprise of the internal candidates when each of them walked into the room and saw one of their peers—the other high school principal—sitting as a member of the panel. So much for their colleagues not knowing they'd applied for the open position! Then, back at school after the 2 days of interviews were over, the PTA president (a panel member) announced to the school governance group, composed of faculty, administrators, parents, and students, that she knew who she wanted to be the next principal, and she was going to call her friend, school board member Jane Doe, and tell her! So much for the interview proceedings being kept confidential! So much for school board members sticking to policy issues and staying out of personnel matters!

The candidate chosen by the area superintendent for the position was not the first (or even the second) choice of the community panel. Two parent panelists felt afterward that the process was rigged, the selection had been predetermined, and their time had been wasted. Even though they had been told their input was but one piece of information to be weighed in making the final decision, they really believed the community should pick its own principal. Therefore, these two individuals felt justified in discussing the process; all the applicants; and the "winner," whom they believed was the wrong choice, with others in the school community, despite having agreed up front to keep the proceedings confidential. They continued to stick thorns in the new principal's side at every opportunity (fortunately, she had thick skin on that side). Certainly, you remember similar spoilsports from games you played as children: They want to change the rules when they aren't winning, they leave in a huff, and they then proceed to bad-mouth the ones who won playing by the rules. It's no wonder that when the well-regarded new principal was promoted to an area office position 3 years later, the area superintendent did not resurrect the community interview panel as part of the process of selecting the new principal for that school. Instead, she found the person she wanted and recommended him to the school board, which appointed him with no further hoopla.

Some might say the preceding example demonstrates why parents should not be part of the personnel selection process. But the area superintendent involved related how other schools' experiences with the same process led to a heightened sense of community and an initiation of a strong partnership between the new principal and parents and staff. And the reality is that not including parents and other stakeholders in selecting school leaders is usually no longer a viable option. Certainly, not all districts use an interview panel in filling leadership positions, and some new principals may not meet members of their new school community until after they are named to the position. Similarly, candidates for a central office administrative job may undergo stakeholder scrutiny in an interview panel, in focus groups—or in the successful candidate's first hour on the job, once it's too late to bow out! So, as you now more nervously anticipate your turn in front of such a panel or your first encounters with members of your new school's or office's stakeholder groups, a few words to the wise might help you view the experience as an adventure. Remember—you can't please everybody, so just please yourself. And as for your personal growth that will come from that adventure, "You can't be brave if you've had only wonderful things happen to you" (Minelli, cited in *Quotable Women*, 1994, p. 26).

And maybe, just maybe, *your* interview experience will be wonderful!

Gather Facts So You Can Protect at Least Part of Your Underbelly

Regardless of whether the selection process for the leadership position you want includes a formal community interview panel, you will be interviewed by various school district personnel. So, do your homework about the school, the school district, the job—be prepared! Here's a few research tips to help you get primed for your interview(s):

- Find out the demographic profile of the student population.
    - ◆ How many minority students are there, and what minorities are represented?
    - ◆ How many students with limited English proficiency attend the school? What are the dominant non-English languages?
    - ◆ What percentage of students come from single-parent households?
    - ◆ What percentage of families are itinerant?
    - ◆ How many students qualify for free and reduced-price lunch?
    - ◆ What are the school's or district's suspension and expulsion rates?
    - ◆ What is the school's or district's dropout rate?

- ◆ If it's a high school, how many students typically proceed to college or other postsecondary education? How many seek vocational training in high school?
- ◆ If it's an elementary school, is before- and after-school child care offered at the school? If so, how many students participate?
- Find out about special programs at the school or in the district, as applicable.
  - ◆ What vocational curriculum opportunities are offered?
  - ◆ What continuum of special education services is offered?
  - ◆ What programs for high-achieving or gifted students exist? For students at risk of dropping out?
  - ◆ What faculty mentoring programs are in place?
  - ◆ What interdisciplinary and/or team-teaching models are being practiced?
- Find out about the school's or district's recent performance on standardized tests. How does this school or district compare with others in the district/region/state?
- Visit the school's facility if you're seeking a school-based administrative position or find out about the facility if you can't go there in person.
  - ◆ How old is the building? When was it last renovated (or is it due for renovation)?
  - ◆ Is the facility overcrowded? If so, are portable classrooms in use? (How many?)
- How does the facility compare to others in the district?
- Find out about any hot issues regarding *anything* in the school or district.
- Learn the recent history of administrators at that school.
  - ◆ Why is the current leadership position open?
  - ◆ How many other administrators are at the school? How long has each been at that school?
- Check the newspapers: Has the school or district received any recent positive or negative publicity from the press?

- Find out what you can about parental and community involvement at the school or in the district.
  - ◆ What does the PTA do? Is there a town, city, or county coalition of PTAs?
  - ◆ How active are local businesses in the school or district? Does the school or district have one or more formal "business partners"?

By doing your homework, you will have gathered as much information as possible about the culture of the position before you have to match your answers to surprise questions. And if it turns out that you will experience a community interview panel as part of the selection process, asking these questions in advance will give you a better feel for that part of the game:

- Who will be on the panel, and how were they selected?
- Where did the questions originate?
- What information will panel members have about you?
- Will you be allowed to ask questions of the panel members?
- What is the time frame for the interview (so you won't use up too much time answering one question)?

Of course, what you really want to know about any type of interview situation is—what are they going to ask me? Won't the diverse stakeholders have different and possibly conflicting hidden agendas? How will I know what to say to address all those agendas? Interview questions are often generic. Typically, they require persons in the hot seat to tell about personal and professional strengths, to give examples of accomplishments, to describe management and communication styles (especially in "what if" situations), and to identify short- and long-term career goals. As for hidden agendas, you can bet every person interviewing you has his or her own image of the type of individual wanted (and not wanted) in the job and his or her own idea of the right (and wrong) answers to the questions. Unless you are a mind reader, there is no way to uncover hidden agendas. So the best—and only—solution is for you to answer each question as well as you can. Be yourself. Speak for yourself. If they don't want you, you don't want to be there.

THE BOTTOM LINE

"Life is what happens when you are busy making other plans" (Talmadge, cited in *Quotable Women*, 1994, p. 14). If you really want to become a principal or move to another leadership position, you are the only one who can make it happen. Don't lose focus and get busy doing other things, making other plans. Don't be sloppy in marketing yourself on paper. Don't be lazy in preparing for your interview. And don't worry about the competition! It's the thoroughness of your preparation and the confidence in your attitude that are the keys to selling yourself in your cover letter and résumé, to impressing the interviewer or interview panel, and to emerging victorious from the principal selection process. Earlier chapters have stressed the importance of cultivating a relationship with a mentor who can not only be a source of great wisdom as you face your early challenges on the job (if you get the job), but whose behind-the-scenes recommendation of you may also give you the final boost above the other contenders. Be positive, too, that the people you list as references will give you a good reference. In the end, though, whether you land your principalship is up to you and nobody else. Go for it!

REFERENCES

Black, S. (1998). Parent support: Research suggests how to keep "parent involvement" from turning into "parent interference." *American School Board Journal, 185*(4), 50-53.

Quotable women: A collection of shared thoughts. (1994). Philadelphia: Running Press Book Publishers.

Webster's ninth new collegiate dictionary. (1985). Springfield, MA: Merriam-Webster.

9

Winning a Race
Without a Finish Line

Changing the Organization
Without Alienating the Culture

*It must be considered that there is nothing more difficult
to carry out, nor more doubtful of success, nor more
dangerous to handle, than to initiate a new order of
things.*

—Machiavelli, *The Prince*

ABOUT THIS CHAPTER

Although we proceed from the assumption that people are fundamentally different in many ways, in the overall *culture* of schools and school districts, there are strong, albeit discrete, similarities. The more we understand and adapt to the patterns of school culture, the better we can make those patterns work effectively for us. In previous chapters, we've examined the culture in which effective school leaders work and how important it is to understand and integrate the culture so that you can play appropriate roles, adopt proper techniques, and use the culture to your *advantage*—as a tool—rather than a *disadvantage*—as a burden. We've also looked at the distinct, but usually coactive, roles of leader and manager in school cultures. This chapter will examine how effective principals/leaders/ managers can bring about change in schools without alienating or insulting the culture.

REFLECTIVE POINT

A number of years ago—many pundit trends ago in one of the continuous cycles of education reform—the quest du jour was whether formal education was really necessary for our nation's children. During that particular era, the early 1970s, the following statement was published:

> Everyone learns to speak, to think, to love, to feel, to play, to curse, to politick, and to work without interference from a teacher. Even children who are under a teacher's care day and night are no exception to the rule. Orphans, idiots, and schoolteachers sons learn most of what they learn outside the "educational" process planned for them. (Illick, 1971, p. 78)

Gosh, I thought I learned it all in kindergarten! Well, anyway, although it may be professional heresy to agree with the author of that 1971 proclamation, you might want to ask yourself, where do or where did I learn to be an effective principal/leader/manager? Clearly, all of us—in our formal K-12 schooling and undergraduate and graduate work—learned and matured under the helpful, watchful eyes of teachers. But we learned an awful lot from the nonschool environment around us. It's a combination of both our formal and informal education that opens the numerous avenues of thought and process and action that can make one effective. Anthony Jay said, "The only real training for leadership is leadership." Harold Geneen, founder of MCI Communications, stated, "Leadership is practiced not so much in words as in attitude and in actions." Mark Twain wrote, "I never let my schooling interfere with my education." The best remark may in fact be Yogi Berra's, "Half of the game is 90% mental" (cited in Robins, 1999).

Now, is there a problem with education as it exists today? Can you transform the strictly management paradigm into which school leaders seem to have fallen to a leadership/management paradigm and start practicing "attitude" *and* "actions" as Geneen suggests? Can you demonstrate to the Mark Twains of today that schooling *enhances* education? Can you reduce the number of Berra's "mental" exercises we go through each year with actual changes others can see?

TWEAKING THE CULTURE IS OKAY: THE TWO SIDES OF CHANGE

This chapter is about change and how leadership coexists with management to bring about effective change. Clearly, the school reform movement that was kicked off with the publication of *A Nation at Risk* (National Commission on Excellence in Education, 1983) has been the most sustained, concerted national effort to change the central core of assumptions and structures of public schools. Since that 1983 publication, "The country has been searching for some magical way to reform and restructure public schools. We have tried—and are still trying—all sorts of alchemical nostrums we hope will turn our educationally ladened school into schools of educational gold" (Evans, 1993, p. 28).

Because the practice of effective leadership in school administration is *both* an art and a science, then education change should also be practiced as both an art and a science. We often view change strictly as something that is managed or decreed into place. That's the scientific side of change, which includes such things as processes, measurement, tools, structures, and procedures. And to bring about change, we need people to implement our new science. We need people to fall in line behind our new management initiative. So, we look at the potential implementers of change and construct rules, regulations, policies, and procedures for all to readily adopt and follow. Our mistake—too often, we tend to view our implementers as one body as opposed to many individual bodies. We forget that people are different from one another, and no amount of hassling or "management" is going to change them. Nor is there any reason to change them, because their individual differences are inherently good, not bad. "People are different in fundamental ways. They *want* different things; they have different motives, purposes, aims,

Figure 9.1.

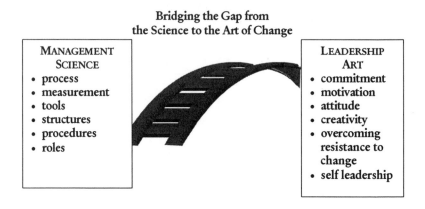

Bridging the Gap from
the Science to the Art of Change

MANAGEMENT SCIENCE	LEADERSHIP ART
• process	• commitment
• measurement	• motivation
• tools	• attitude
• structures	• creativity
• procedures	• overcoming resistance to change
• roles	• self leadership

values, needs, drives, impulses, and urges. They *believe* differently: they think, cognize, conceptualize, perceive, understand, comprehend, and cogitate differently" (Keirsey & Bates, 1984, p. 2). If you understand the important patterns of those differences, then you can make that understanding work productively for change. "History will judge leaders on—among other things—how well they understand the traditional framework of values, and on how they renew the tradition by adapting it to contemporary dilemmas" (Gardner, 1990, p. 106). Nothing is really more basic than that.

So, now we need to infuse the art side of change. To ensure that change *can* take place, and probably *will* take place, you need buy-in, commitment, attitude, and creativity from your potential implementers. You need to build a bridge between resistance to change and commitment to change—a bridge between seeing change as a decree, and seeing change as an opportunity for all implementers to be self-leaders. You're only tweaking the overall culture here, only working with people—not concrete structures. So, there are *two* sides of organizational change, whether it's school site based or district based. As depicted in Figure 9.1, one side is about management (the science of change) and the other side is about leadership (the art of change).

If you want to be a positive change agent for your school or district, you must be able to implement both sides of the change paradigm. You must be an effective leader as well as an effective manager. And you must be willing and able to create excellence through creativity and invention as opposed to "this is the way we've always done it" or becoming ineffective by continuously synthesizing existing ideas.

Research and theory on change and school reform provide one foundation for practice. Equally important, however, to becoming effective is craft knowledge, that is, the body of knowledge accumulated through practice and transmitted from one administrator to another—with a minimum of folklore. Effective change management and the ability to practice leadership require both a commitment to lifelong learning and a dedication to reflective practice.

Leadership as a component of administration has been addressed in literally thousands of articles and hundreds of books. Research studies on this topic have targeted a number of variables, including personal traits, on-the-job behaviors, motives, and power. Unfortunately, the findings have been inclusive, and at times even contradictory (Yuki, 1989). A disjunction between theory and practice has been a long-standing problem in education administration (Kowalski, 1999). Effective leaders use all of the inherent and learned senses available to them. Common sense may be, in fact and in practice, the most important. Where does one get common sense? Can it be learned in the classroom? From books? From mentors? Some of it can, but most common sense comes from observation— from becoming streetwise through seeing, listening, and feeling.

MANAGING CHANGE THROUGH LEADERSHIP

"Leaders function not as gatekeepers but as door openers, bent on widening participation. They also insist that others take ownership [self-leadership]" (Mathews, 1996, p. 68). As professional educators, we do an outstanding job of instilling in our teaching and administrative employees a feeling of ownership. A principal refers to his or her school as "my school," and a teacher almost always identifies his or her working space as "my classroom." Experienced principals have heard such terms as "my desk," "my bulletin board," "my file cabinet," "my bookshelf" whenever they moved a teacher from one room to another. This feeling of ownership is good and needs to be sustained. But when ownership in one thing is not exchanged for ownership of something of equal value, then human resistance is normal and should be anticipated. During periods of change, human resistance to change frequently becomes magnified or intensified. Security is a basic human need, and organizational changes tend to create a sense of insecurity by replacing the known with the unknown. In any organization, people are resistant to change because they fear that the proposed changes will

- Require them to learn new skills, develop new relationships, and devise new means to manage their environment that may be less successful than the ones they are used to, e.g., shortened or lengthened class meeting times, working with Betty's team rather than Harry's, a classroom on the north side of the building instead of the south side, etc.
- Result in the loss of something they value, e.g., power, influence, a window, a file cabinet, that special bulletin board, a planning period just before, or right after, lunch, etc. (Dresser, 1986, p. 19)

People in the education profession generally consider themselves as specialists who have extensive training in a fairly narrow field and less flexibility in the kinds of work they feel they can accomplish successfully. They often feel vulnerable to the real or perceived politics of change, and are uncertain that their bosses understand the complexity of the proposed change or share their commitment to particular programs and events, much less to the hard work they've put into building what they see as right, educationally sound—and set in stone. Status quo is the most comfortable—*this* day's rules, regulations, policies, and procedures are okay.

All great performance involves improving the ways one achieves the result—better methods, better means to the goal. But means tend to triumph over ends. Form triumphs over spirit. People become prisoners of their procedures. The means and methods were originally designed to achieve some specific end, but when circumstances change and new means are called for, it turns out that the old ones have become sacrosanct; the means have become ends in themselves—no longer effective perhaps, but enshrined. People forget what they set out to do. It happens all the time. So the mature organization ends up with a web of customs, procedures, written and unwritten rules that is extremely hard to cut through. (Gardner, 1990, p. 123)

Because changes in any area of the school or district threaten to upset the intricate systems and networks individuals have built, school personnel are apt to perceive that their personal success and security are closely tied to the status quo (Dresser, 1986, p. 20). Based on this perspective and the sincere conviction that their work, as currently defined, is critical, these faculty and staff members typically exhibit strong resistance to change. It takes only a few resisters to sabotage a school administrator's plans to bring about change. It's the fear of the unknown that underlies most change resistance. Making the unknown known and completely unveiling the rationale behind the proposed change are the keys to reducing resistance.

So, with these thoughts in mind, *leading* change should be fairly easy. Let's see now—we'll reduce resistance by making the unknown known. Assure involved personnel that their security isn't in jeopardy and that their bosses clearly understand how important they and their programs have been to the district and community. We'll promise them that there won't be any losses of things they value, that any new skills required for success they already possess, and that developing new relationships is really fun. And finally, we'll assure them that they will love their new environment. It sounds easy enough—sounds good, in fact! You're leading, not managing. This is why the "art" of leadership as opposed to the "science" of management is important.

Think of teachers, secretaries, custodians, food workers, bus drivers, and so on as "managers" for a moment. In his work on the role of process consultation in organization development, Edgar Schein pointed out some reasons that managers need assistance from others (consultants, in his framework, or leaders, in ours) to address organizational problems. Managers often know that a problem exists, but often they don't know exactly what the problem is— they may be too mired in the problem to actually recognize it. So, even though managers may honestly want to address existing problems, not only do they need help in knowing how to improve their organization, they first need help identifying exactly what the problems are. Schein was explaining how an outside process consultant can step into an organization and guide its managers to recognize and diagnose problems, come up with a solution from a number of alternatives, and then decide on the course the organization will pursue. But he could also have been discussing the critical role that leaders play in working with managers to identify needed change—and getting those who will implement the change (i.e., the managers) to be part of the problem solving and decision making involved in bringing about the necessary change—ultimately making the implementers of change into self-leaders (Shafritz & Russell, 1997).

One of the ways people successfully adapt to change is through active involvement in the process. Affected personnel should be involved in the change process from the earliest planning stages. Through their active participation, they can receive the maximum amount of information about, and experience with, the potential change, and provide valuable feedback. If they discover genuine, rather than imagined, problems with the plan, their expertise can be used to make necessary adjustments (Dresser, 1986, p. 19). By involving personnel as implementers, you will be creating a cadre of self-leaders. Successful and effective change now becomes probable because previously potential resisters have now developed a sense of ownership in the project.

THE BOTTOM LINE

A year or so ago, the following appeared in the *Wall Street Journal*. It's exactly on target—it's an excellent "bottom line":

> I have been lucky to have worked for two bosses who were leaders more than managers. The first went by the rule, "If it isn't broke, break it anyway." He loved throwing dozens of ideas into the air and then waiting to see which would fly. He could be erratic, and he didn't forgive mistakes easily, but he was a magnet for attracting talent. His curiosity and excitement about trying new things rubbed off on others, and he made the people who worked for him feel special.
>
> The second leader was steadier and quieter but also driven by a standard of excellence and ability to challenge

others to do their very best. Keenly observant, he seemed to always know who was good at what and how to keep fiercely competitive players on the same team. By example, he taught me not to be swayed by critics from doing what I thought best.

Leaders . . . typically inspire those who follow them to take risks and do more than they ever thought possible. Leaders set steep goals and then convince employees that while failure is permissible, so is success. (Hymowitz, 1998, p. B1)

What the author of the excerpt above has observed is fundamental. Effective principals practice both the art and the science of change leadership/management. Effective principals demonstrate an ongoing trust in people and are not afraid to practice calculated risk taking to bring about effective change. Education change leaders need to seek leadership positions with the mission of determining education's direction and pace. Who's going to do it if you don't?

A CONCLUDING THOUGHT

Constraints under which you must operate include the expectations of individuals and groups both inside and outside the school and school district, fishbowl visibility, pressures of time, vested interest groups, risk, and possible dead ends. The principalship is a race without a finish line, but the starting line is clear—increasing your influence and power, achieving more visibility, and constantly building a positive aggregate impression will get you the green flag to proceed with the day-to-day problem solving inherent in any principalship.

Each year, the middle management position of principal has taken on more and more complicated characteristics. Today's principal works in the center of a society that in itself is complicated and demanding. Although most of these demands originate from legitimate groups—school boards, parent organizations, advisory councils, unions, and legislatures—ever more frequently you hear from student protesters, minority activists, street gangs, textbook vigilantes, and single-issue parent and political groups. Effective principals, to remain effective, deal with the formal bureaucracy as well as the procedural surprises and volatile demands of a litigious society and an abundance of quasi-legitimate groups. Effective principals are effective leaders and managers and, when allowed to, can easily respond to a multitude of demands.

So, we need principals who aren't afraid to talk about what's good in education and who will forcefully counteract those who seek notoriety through inventing and reinventing what's not good about education. Education leaders, from the superintendent to the principal to the teacher, must step forward with conviction, willingness to take risk, and the smart-sense to win education back from the political arena. We need education leaders who will help professional educators control their environment rather than submissively pass control to others. Harry Truman noted, "In periods where there is no leadership, society stands still. Progress is made when courageous, skillful leaders seize the opportunity to change things for the better" (cited in Robins, 1999). Knowing the *culture* in which you are attempting to be courageous will provide you with one of the tools you'll need to practice effective leadership, management, and change. That's what this book has been about.

As we move through the 21st century, we need districtwide administrators who will allow principals and teachers to be inventive, set the pace, fulfill visions, and make mistakes on the way to success. We need districtwide administrators who will allow principals and teachers to dream, to ask why not, and to explain what things could be as opposed to "this is the way we've always done it." We need districtwide administrators who will allow principals and teachers to see beyond the trees and even beyond the forest—to see the fertile ground waiting for change.

This book is dedicated to all the people who respond to *your* new ideas and actions with a simple comment, "Try it," and to all the people who allow you to smile and even laugh as you go about the critical business of educating kids. Finally, and most important, this book is especially dedicated to you.

Karl Wallenda stated, "Being on the tightrope is living, everything else is waiting" (cited in Robins, 1999). Go for it!

REFERENCES

Dresser, S. G. (1986, September). Managing change effectively. *Executive Update*, pp. 19-21.

Evans, C. (1993, December 8). Magnet schools matter. *Education Week*, p. 28.

Gardner, J. W. (1990). *On leadership*. New York: Free Press.

Hymowitz, C. (1998, December 8). In the lead: Some managers are more than bosses—They're leaders. *Wall Street Journal*, p. B1.

Illick, I. (1971). *Deschooling society*. New York: Harper & Row.

Keirsey, D., & Bates, M. (1984). *Please understand me: Character and temperament types*. Del Mar, CA: Prometheus Nemesis Book Company.

Kowalski, T. J. (1999). *The school superintendent: Theory, practice, and cases*. Upper Saddle River, NJ: Prentice Hall.

Mathews, D. (1996). *Is there a public for public schools?* Dayton, OH: Kettering Foundation Press.

National Commission on Excellence in Education. (1983). *A nation at risk*. Washington, DC: Government Printing Office.

Robins, G. (1999, December 20). *Good Quotations by famous people*. http://www.cs.virginia.edu/~robins/quotes/html

Shafritz, J. M., & Russell, E. W. (1997). *Introducing public administration*. New York: Addison Wesley Educational Publishers.

Yuki, G. A. (1989). *Leadership in organizations* (2nd ed.). Upper Saddle River, NJ: Prentice Hall.

Index